First published in Great Britain in 2021 by
Laurence King Publishing
an imprint of The Orion Publishing Group Ltd
Carmelite House, 50 Victoria Embankment
London EC4Y 0DZ

An Hachette UK Company

1 3 5 7 9 10 8 6 4 2

ISBN 978 1 91394 711 8

Design by Alexandre Coco
Cover design by Pentagram
Printed in China by C&C Offset Printing Co Ltd

Laurence King Publishing is committed to
ethical and sustainable production. We are
proud participants in The Book Chain Project®
bookchainproject.com

www.laurenceking.com
www.orionbooks.co.uk

THE HAPPY WRITING BOOK

Discover the Positive Power of Creative Writing

Elise Valmorbida

Laurence King Publishing

HAPPY BEGINNINGS

HAPPY MIDDLES

HAPPY ENDS

I DARE YOU

I've been teaching creative writing – classes, workshops, mentoring – for more than 20 years. I love teaching and believe that in order to be a good teacher I must be a good student. I constantly learn from my students, and I delight in responding to the challenges they give me.

Over the decades, I've noticed several recurring issues: pesky problems, classic hopes, common fears and dreams. I've also noticed how those of us who stick at the practice of creative writing find new kinds of happiness in our lives. Sometimes it's the euphoria of an inspirational moment, the gratification of being published or winning praise. But it's the lasting kind of happiness that most interests me. It is slow to build. Uneven, but certain. It happens piece by tiny piece, like a mosaic. It emerges from ways of seeing, and ways of doing. With time, creative writing can enhance wellbeing, which can enhance creative writing, which can enhance wellbeing...

Such teaching-learning prompted me to write the first pages of this book more than 15 years ago, and I have been adding to it slowly ever since.

Reflecting an archetypal story structure, *The Happy Writing Book* is divided into three parts: beginnings, middles and ends. This structure is not about levels or stages. Creativity does not move in straight lines or regular steps. You can dip in at random, or read from start to finish.

Happy Beginnings – incitement, excitement – are about overcoming obstacles, being prepared, nurturing ideas, breaking blocks and letting go. Whether you're a seasoned writer or a newcomer, you'll find chapters here to open your mind and open your heart.

Happy Middles – complication, concentration – are about being under way, paying attention, fuelling up, developing the craft. Dive in here for plenty of *how-to* tips, some literal and some lateral.

Happy Ends – resolution, resilience – are about goals, persevering, finishing and some of the life-enhancing outcomes that spring from creative writing practice. In this part of the book you'll find suggestions of *how-to*, and *why-to*.

Some chapters are packed with spurs to action; others are more about thinking in fresh ways. Some tasks will take you ten minutes, job done. Some exercises are designed for ritual repetition, little and often. Others are reliable writing techniques that you can return to whenever you need them. (As I do.) There are ideas you'll enjoy pondering, letting them settle, taking your time; you might find yourself thinking them through for a week, and playing with them months later. You'll be offered suggestions, and contradictory suggestions. You can pick and mix. For every person who flourishes with a deadline, there's someone else who wilts at the prospect. But sometimes habits and aversions are worth confronting – how else to expand your repertoire?

Insights from other disciplines have percolated into my teaching and writing practice, so they make an appearance here. I've learned from doing tai chi, film-making, communications consultancy, art and design. I've studied languages and philosophy. Psychology, music and neuroscience inspire me too.

You'll see that I refer to all forms of creative writing, although my guidance leans a little towards prose, and towards English language and literature. I look to the wisdom of famous and unfamous people, some of whom died centuries ago. I quote student-writers, friends and peers. I draw on personal material too, sharing insight from my own experiences as teacher, student and practitioner.

Forget the plodding instruction manual – think 100 parcels of inspiration and provocation.

This book is for you if you wrote funny poems when you were nine years old, or you kept a stormy journal in your teen years, or the last truly creative work you produced was at school, and you remember how much fun it was but you haven't done it since. Perhaps you've been persuaded that you're 'not creative' and you simply want to realize your expressive potential through writing. Perhaps you wax a bit lyrical when you email your bank about a glitch in their service, or you loiter with intent around the blogosphere. Perhaps you want to tackle a significant project – say, your memoir or family history – and you want to write it well.

Equally, this book is for you if you wield words for a living. You may have work that's published or produced, and you want to explore new directions or improve your creative stroke. Writers of all kinds can get stuck. You may be writing like a wild thing, just for the love of it, but you're not sure how to make progress. You may be involved in a different creative practice – visual art, film-making, marketing, fashion, design, dance – and you're keen to extend your storytelling powers. Whatever your art, *The Happy Writing Book* is for you too.

This is a practical writing guide, but it's brimming with ideas to enhance wellbeing, not just creative output. The angle might be something as small and rich as *noticing*. Or tackling an unhelpful habit. It might be about embracing skills, conquering fears or building confidence. What about cultivating curiosity? Creating for pleasure? You can use specific writing tasks to spark positive change in yourself or in the wider world. Throughout, I encourage you to think well, nurture your imagination and make the most of your inner resources.

Some of the strategies offered here involve action and discipline. Some of the concepts are simply affirmative; you can read them and do no homework at all. If you take the suggested techniques and insights to heart, you will be a more confident, more creative, more effective writer – and this can have positive impacts on your life.

Whatever you do, I dare you to relish reading, writing and living.

Here and there in Old English poetry, you'll chance upon a beautiful phrase for storytelling. The warrior Beowulf *unlocked his word-hoard*. The poet Widsith *unlocked his word-hoard*. Wisdom herself *unlocked her word-hoard*. It's a concept loaded with treasure and generosity. I encourage you to unlock your word-hoard.

HAPPY BEGINNINGS

Think incitement, excitement.
Happy Beginnings are all about
overcoming obstacles, dismantling
doubt, sparking inspiration, letting
yourself go... Whether you're a
seasoned writer or a newcomer,
you'll find chapters here to open
your mind and open your heart.

1
WHY WRITE?

My mother taught me to write when I was about three years old. I was so excited that I went off and wrote all over the wallpaper. I had no intention of being destructive or seeking attention. I was just thrilled at this new grown-up power and wanted to exercise it. Thinking about it now, I realize there was a sense of magic in the very act of writing: getting something invisible out of my whirligig head, into my hand, translating it through an implement, onto a surface, making visible marks that others could read and understand.

That was writing.

Then there was creative writing: the enchantment of words, shaping poems, inventing voices and scenes, crafting stories. *Someone* made the magic that emanated from books. Writers. Many of those writers were also illustrators. Much of my childhood was spent reading, writing, drawing and painting. I have been torn between the lures of visual and verbal magic ever since, but it looks like writing has won.

Creative writing is a kind of happy addiction. You might start out feeling that you can just experiment. Or it's peer group pressure (other people are writing and you don't want to be left out). You think you can resist or succumb whenever you feel like it. There's a hint of dangerous glamour about it – you've seen those damaged-looking individuals who win big prizes and record-breaking advances.

Whether you're feeling vulnerable, or strong as a cockroach, don't fool yourself: it is an addiction. Writing is stronger than you are. It starts out being fun and interesting, but soon it becomes a gnawing need, an insatiable craving – and you will do almost anything to satisfy it.

You have been warned.

So why write? Apart from trying to earn a living, George Orwell identifies four great urges for writing prose. He doesn't call it addiction. He implies that writers have the free will to choose, because he calls these four great urges *motives*.

Can you admit to 'sheer egoism'? Do you feel 'aesthetic enthusiasm'? Are you susceptible to 'historical impulse' or 'political purpose – using the word "political" in the widest possible sense'? To some degree, Orwell argues, all writers are motivated by a desire for attention, the pleasure to be gained from different kinds of beauty (even from the arrangement of words), the value of sharing experiences, the search for truth, and aspirations to change the world by influencing people to think or feel in a certain way.

If you share Orwell's declared motives, you have the makings of a writer, if you're not one already. If you can be as honest as Orwell, as committed as he was to sincerity and truth, then you're off to a flying start.

Why write? Enjoy taking time to ponder your own answer to this question.

2
IT HASN'T ALL BEEN DONE BEFORE

At Tate Modern, you'll find an elegantly engraved faux-marble ruin entitled THE WORLD HAS BEEN EMPTY SINCE THE ROMANS. It's as if the fragments of an antique frieze, the heavy freight of the past, have been pieced together to hang above our heads. It says it all. Everything has been said and done. But that did not deter Ian Hamilton Finlay, the artist who created this compelling contemporary artwork, from saying and doing a new thing.

Students of creative writing ask if this or that story hasn't all been done before.

'Of course it has,' I say. 'How many star-cross'd lovers stories are there?'

But that didn't put Shakespeare off. In fact he was inspired by it. He based his plot on an English narrative poem that was inspired by an earlier Italian story, itself inspired by tragic love stories from antiquity. This weighty recycled heritage didn't deter the creators of *West Side Story*. Nor did it get in the way of countless *Romeo-and-Juliet*-inspired operas, ballets and songs. Film-makers return to the romance again and again, making it new each time – happily, Franco Zeffirelli and Baz Luhrmann didn't hold back.

If Shakespeare is the greatest writer in English, surely after Shakespeare there's no point?

What if Mark Twain had said that, or Jane Austen? Imagine if Virginia Woolf and Toni Morrison had opted for silence, if Michael Ondaatje had kept himself to himself, if T.S. Eliot and Samuel Beckett hadn't bothered. None of these writers threw their pens away because life was too dark in the shadow of the greats who preceded them. What kind of ego does it take to compare yourself with historical greatness anyway?

A happier ego is one that says: I will write. I have my reasons. What I write may shine; it may not. But the experience is worth it. And the end-product is worth it, even if I am the only reader. I will not compare myself to Rupi Kaur or Margaret Atwood – this is not a competition. I will find my own writing voice. I will write because I want to. Because it opens my soul, wakes up my brain, makes my heart sing, connects me more powerfully to the world.

It hasn't all been done before. There's more to do. Write your creative contribution to the world. It will be uniquely yours, something only you can make, because there's only one of you.

3
NEVER MIND UBIQUITY

We are pelted with words. They fall out of newspapers, run along the uprisers of subway steps, flash from electrified screens. They burn and sting and distract and dazzle. They stick to the soft matter of our brains. Why on earth should we add more? Surely we should exercise a little self-restraint and allow the world's population of words to settle at this already overcrowded level?

No. We're not about to let ubiquity get in the way.

Every day, every hour, every minute, every moment, the world changes. And as long as the world changes, there is something new to perceive, something new to make sense of, something new to express.

Change keeps writers busy going forward. There's nothing like a revolution, a scientific breakthrough or a shocking crime to get the ink flowing. But change can work backwards too. Think how much new writing is spawned by an archaeological discovery, the release of top-secret files, the unearthing of a long-lost manuscript, the rewriting of history through new lenses.

And the changes don't have to be newsworthy. The 'archaeological discovery' can be a personal treasure hidden in a cupboard. The 'top-secret files' can be the military records of your forebears. The 'long-lost manuscript' can be your own childhood diary.

As long as we exist, and perceive, and experience change, there is absolutely no reason not to write. To put it positively, the world now is not what it was a moment ago. Add your words to it. There is always something new to say.

4
SHORT IS SWEET

You don't have to have a big story to tell. It doesn't have to be the magnum opus, the history of the universe or the family bible. Don't worry about whether your words are grand enough, or if what you have to say is important enough. The minute you worry about writing big, you'll be writing badly, putting on a posh voice.

Write as an exercise, just as an athlete does warm-ups and a visual artist does sketches. You'll develop writing muscles. Then you need to keep them strong and toned, which takes regular practice.

Start small. Think inconsequential.

Find the words to encapsulate one emotion you've felt, or one complete thought. The Roman poet Catullus (first century BCE) conveys so much in this timeless poem, a concentrated couplet:

> *I hate and I love. Why do I do this, you might ask.*
> *I don't know, but I feel it happening and it's excruciating.*

Try your hand at a 16-line rap about something that gets to you, written from the first-person point of view, in the present tense. Or dip your toe into Instapoetry, a few short, direct, shareable lines about something that matters to you. You could write a haiku capturing a moment, using just three lines (five syllables/seven syllables/five syllables).

Here seventeenth-century poet Matsuo Bashō shows us that short is not just sweet, it can be sublime:

> *Ah, silent stillness*
> *Seeping deep into the rocks*
> *A cicada's cry.*

5
DIVINE COINCIDENCE

Certainty is overrated. Being uncertain is fine. Don't worry if your thoughts feel vague, if you don't have enough 'material'. Once you start putting pen to paper, or tapping the keyboard, you'll see that details come.

At first, like an ant.

Just the one.

Then, another ant.

Two tiny details that bring life to your spacious abstractions.

—Is that a third ant?

Keep writing. Or do something else altogether, but notice that more ants appear, drawn into the void by those first few pioneers. Before you know it, your writing is a busy little world of ant-trails and cargo systems and nest-building and connections.

Such elaboration doesn't happen unless you've got something started. Those first few written thoughts are laden with formic pheromones that attract other thoughts, then more thoughts...

Once your work is under way, your eyes and ears are open to details that will inform and enrich your writing. Your perceptive powers will be tuned to your project's needs.

Tell people a little (not too much) about your work in progress, and they will spontaneously provide for you – they'll send you links to articles, interviews, websites, events, sources of inspiration you couldn't have imagined back in the one-ant moment. All of this is fertile material.

And then there's luck. If you have a specific writing project on the go, you'll find that the universe throws you juicy titbits from any direction – relevant facts and welcome insights that seem to be made just for your story, or the right word, overheard, for your poem. Your days are peppered with these happy coincidences. You pounce on them. The world is suddenly connected in marvellous new ways.

Catalyze coincidence and connection. How? By starting.

6
YOU HAVE NOTHING TO SAY?

Once upon a time, I signed up for a short course in creative writing. It was a struggle to get there after a long day at work. I was usually late. The teacher set us assignments that I attempted, but not always. At the end of each class, a few of us wandered to the pub nearby. The literary discussion continued late into the night.

When the term ended, we decided to keep on meeting to read out work and offer each other feedback, without a tutor.

At our first tutorless meeting, one person turned up with his half-finished third unpublished novel. Another brought one of her many short stories. Another had a themed collection of short stories under way. And so on.

I had nothing. I needed a tutor to set me writing tasks. I hoped that inspiration might come. It didn't. I figured that I was still useful to the others because I could offer feedback. But week after week I felt inadequate. I felt like a fraud.

Eventually I confessed.

'I know I want to write, but I don't know what.'

The writer who was halfway through his third unpublished novel simply said to me: 'Remember that homework you did, describing a place, I think it was in Italy? That sounded interesting. Why don't you do something with that?'

It was all I needed.

A green light.

I returned to that random creative writing exercise and started to flesh out a character who might live in that place. I began tapping into my Italian roots. The following week I read out a fragment of text that grew into the first chapter of my first novel.

That writer-friend now has several published novels to his name, our writing group continues, and to this day I am grateful to him for giving me that green light.

I tell this story to my creative writing students because in every class there's at least one person who really wants to write, but they don't know *what*. Like me all those years ago.

If you have a wise writer-friend, don't be shy. Ask for a prompt, a way to start.

Or try your hand at the news.

Choose an article that catches your attention and makes an impression on you. Use it as a springboard for an entirely new story. Don't feel you have to stick to the journalistic facts. Feel free to extrapolate and explore.

You might dream up what happened before, or after, the reported event. Think consequence.

You might decide to see things from the perspective of one of the characters inside the story, or at the story's edges. Imagine being the player who scored that goal. Imagine being the mother of that criminal.

Imagine being the world's biggest toad.

We might read the story as an email exchange, a fictive diary or a witness statement. It might unfold as an epic narrative poem. We might 'hear' it as spoken words – perhaps as gossip, a prophecy, a confession, a troubadour's song.

With the reassurance of truth at a story's centre, your imagination often ranges more freely. The beauty of using a news story is that it already has a beginning, a middle and an end. What you do with the story's themes, sequence, perspectives or form will be your unique imagination at work.

Tackle this task, and you'll see that you have something to say.

7
THIS PRECIOUS NOW

My friend is late. I don't mind. I arrive at the café, knowing that I have my notebook in my pocket. I remember a stray thought I had this morning. Something about it tugs at me. It's worth making a note while I remember it. I'm not sure what it means. But, like things in the attic, you never know when stray thoughts will come in handy.

Then I sit and observe. I write about the sensations that come together to create this present time. The competing smells of bleach and chips and coffee. The clatter of cutlery. The grubby edge on the waitress's white bra that shows when she lifts her arm to grab the cashier's attention. Outside, a small brown dog scuds along the pavement like a paper bag.

These things may or may not matter, but what does matter is that I am aware, in the moment. It's like an active meditation in this scattering, distracting world.

A Japanese friend of mine says: *ichi go, ichi e*. Literally, it means *one time, one meeting*. It's the idea of valuing a person, an experience, as unique. This – this now – is precious and never to be repeated.

Once you let yourself be a writer, you learn to love This Precious Now. You appreciate life's variety of limbo and purgatory. You relish all those in-between places and times that used to get written off as losses. Traffic jams, waiting rooms, transit… they are opportunities to perceive or write. Even the most familiar and ordinary situations can become intriguing. You discover aesthetic pleasure in small nothings, significance in random banter overheard on a bus, invaluable detail in a stranger's face.

You are more curious. And more patient. Your perceptions are more intense. And you are never, ever bored.

Attend to it. Open yourself to This Precious Now.

8
FOREIGNERS WELCOME

It was only after I had settled in England that I could properly *see* the cockatoos and spiders of my childhood. But I am twice foreign. I grew up Italian in Australia. I learned ways of thinking and behaving that were sometimes alien to the majority culture. And my head was full of migrant stories, people and places that seemed exotic, yet were utterly familiar – part of me, like my Italian face and surname. Being Italian was not cool. It was just foreign.

The migrant brain is prone to metaphor. Belonging in more than one place, yet not fully belonging anywhere, having distance and perspective, the outsider is perpetually balancing *here* and *there*.

This is not just a matter of geography. The 'places' can be cultural, emotional, perhaps utterly notional. What tales emerge when we journey from one kind of life to another, one identity to another? What happens when we cross borders? Many writers are displaced persons travelling restlessly between different places in their minds. The past can be a foreign country. Freedom, after confinement, can be a wilderness or a wonderland.

For readers, outsiderness is a gift.

We crave to be transported to places that are less well-travelled. We are humanized when we can perceive others with nuance and understanding beyond stereotypes.

For writers, outsiderness is a gift.

Many situations that in everyday life may be seen as disadvantageous – being different, being alone, being in-between – can be surprisingly advantageous. As a writer, that difference is a source of strength.

Cherish your difference. Embrace the outsider within you.

9

INDULGE YOUR PASSIONS

Years ago, I wrote a short story based on a dream I'd scribbled into a notebook. My dream scribble went something like this: *Two JFK lookalikes are in a reality TV show. During their final 'test', a re-enactment of the Dallas motorcade, one gets shot and one survives. Which one is the winner?*

Celebrity and surveillance, it seemed to me, were two sides of the same coin. But I didn't properly *think* this yet. I may have felt it. I didn't know that my disquiet was a preoccupation until I started writing about it. I fed the fascination with intensive research, exploration, imagination. My characters grew and lived lives, and the short story inspired by a dream became chapter one of a novel about celebrity and surveillance.

What will you write about? What matters to you?

Make a list of the topics that keep coming up in your conversations. Books or films or artworks that fascinate you. The values you hold dear. The events that resist easy explanation. The political issues you care about. The person, or people, you think about again and again – perhaps a member of your family, a dear lost soul, an individual who made a big impact on your life.

Your list of pet subjects might include:

- people
- events
- stories
- ideas, beliefs, theories, discoveries
- concerns and issues
- your origins, family, heritage
- your hopes (for yourself, for others)
- your leisure pursuit, interest, expertise
- current sociological trends

Be specific. Once you've made your list, try writing directly about one of your subjects and see where the words take you. The very act of writing is likely to lay your thoughts and feelings bare, revealing new insights. It may put that particular issue to rest, in which case you can get on with something else. Or you can start with a random prompt *(see Chapter 64),* and your obsessions will inevitably work their way through. In other words, you can get your passions and preoccupations out and onto the page unfiltered as a cathartic practice, finding relief through release, or you can distil them into your imaginative creations.

In *Writing Down the Bones*, writer-teacher Natalie Goldberg offers this sound advice:

> *Your main obsessions have power; they are what you will come back to in your writing over and over again. And you'll create new stories around them. So you might as well give in to them. They probably take over your life whether you want them to or not, so you ought to get them to work for you.*

10
IT'S
NOT YOU...

If you write a play, a poem, a song, a short story, a work of fiction or non-fiction, you're creating an artefact.

It's got some of you in it – but it's not you.

If you want to create the best artefact you possibly can, it's unlikely to be effortless from the word go. Sometimes effort is a deterrent, because it can feel like incompetence and vulnerability. Even if you're writing your big life story – *especially* if you're writing your big life story – it can help to think of it as something less important.

Imagine you're learning how to make a piece of furniture.

And then a better piece of furniture.

This piece is elegantly designed, and here is an interesting choice of material, but those unstable joints could be strengthened. This rough surface needs sanding and polishing. Those details feel excessive.

The process of criticism can help us get better at the storytelling craft, although it takes humility and patience. It also takes resilience because, when we write, we draw on personal experience. We need to be tough and talk about whether the language needs polishing, or whether the structure needs strengthening. We do well to separate the artefact from the person who made it.

Show your work to others if you want to see it through their eyes. They might take it apart. It might never come together again. Get your work out there if you want an audience.

Or stash it in a locked drawer if you are your only intended reader. There's nothing wrong with keeping your artefact to yourself. The very act of writing has had its purpose. You've created an object that has some of you in it – but it's not you. How wondrous. How beautiful.

11
THE
IMAGINATION BOX

'I'm not creative,' some people say. 'I don't have an imagination.'

I've heard this from new writers, experienced journalists and concrete thinkers in every field. They find it difficult to *make things up*. They feel stuck on *what happened* or what they know to be true.

I ask them what they are doing next weekend. They tell me about meeting a friend, or going to a party, or travelling abroad. I ask them to describe this event. The friend will need consolation because it's the anniversary of a bereavement, the party will be full of bores and drunks from the office, the trip will be challenging because it's to a troubled country.

Already the person 'without an imagination' has imagined, because none of these events has happened yet.

And without too much effort, this same person can imagine different scenarios: the friend might not turn up at all, the attractive freelancer might be at the party, the trip could be the catalyst for a much-needed career change. This very basic exercise is a reminder that we humans with our big brains are designed to premeditate, to change our plans, to anticipate outcomes, to imagine different possibilities. Imagination keeps us safe. It even keeps us alive.

Until next week happens, next week is a work of imagination. The same can be said about the past.

Think about something significant that's happened to you. Write the story factually, being faithful to the truth in every detail. Pretend it's a witness statement for a court of law. You must not commit perjury. A lawyer will test the veracity of your claims. Guesses must be described as such. Hearsay must be acknowledged as just that. Separate clearly what you *know* to be true, from what you *think* or *feel* is true. Soon you'll realize how much you've heard from other people or imagined. So much of what appears to be objective truth is, in fact, a series of subjective impressions, suppositions and fuzzy memories. So many apparent facts are actually feelings.

Stick with this story of something that happened to you. Now imagine exactly the same event – say, a memorable childhood incident – from your father's or mother's perspective. Describe the school you went to – then describe it from your playground rival's point of view. Imagine how your ex-lover would write about your relationship and why it ended. Your reality looks very different through someone else's eyes. A bit of conflict, or even a divergence of opinion, is a good way to yield a story.

If your true story felt tragic, rewrite it so that it becomes a comedy or a documentary account. If your experience of school or work was boring, retell it so that it sounds bizarre. If your ex-lover is someone you'd like to berate, try writing their compassionate biography instead.

A healthy person who claims to have no imagination has probably just had it boxed in by the discouragements, misreadings or dogmatic pronouncements of others. People in authority can be adept at this. Context matters too – we inherit habits of thought from school, family and the workplace.

It may feel effortful to get your creative spirit out of the box, but it doesn't mean that there's nothing inside. In fact, imagination likes being exposed. The more you nurture it with light and water and air, the more it grows and flourishes. It's never too late.

Scientific studies show that if you cultivate your creativity, you'll be cultivating your happiness too. And it goes both ways. If you cultivate your happiness, you'll be freeing your mind to be more creative.

12
YOU CAN BE ANYTHING YOU LIKE

How much creative pleasure can you have when you bend or break the rules? Think of Shakespeare's male actors performing female roles, being 'women' who disguise themselves as men for good reasons of story – it's a multi-layered celebration of difference and likeness. The ironies depend on our assumptions of what it means to be feminine or masculine. And it isn't necessarily binary.

How much fun can you have with your identity?

Jennie Walker, who penned the novel *24 for 3*, was considered a contender for the Orange Prize for Literature, an award for women writers, until the authorial *she* turned out to be a *he*, the poet and publisher Charles Boyle.

His company, CB Editions, published one of my novels. I know it from him that he loved writing an intimate story entirely in the first person from a woman's point of view. The exploration goes beyond gender.

He wrote in his blog that publishing literature under pen-names (Jennie Walker, Jack Robinson) was 'liberating precisely because they enabled me to sidestep the Charles Boyle I felt a need to distance myself from.'

We are told we can't be things.

You can't be a ballerina because your bones are too big. You can't be an airline pilot because your eyesight is poor. You can't be insured because you're too risky. You can't be a fungus, vegetable or mineral because you're a human.

Humbug!

If you're a writer, you can be a tale-telling dog, a sex slave living in the future, a polar explorer from a hundred years ago, or a sentient can of beans. Write with informed sensitivity, and you can be anything you like. The first permission you need to give yourself is this: you can be a writer.

Here's a workout to flex your writing muscles. Make a list of seven objects that belong to a character you wish to explore. Is this a shopping list? The stash of a thief? Are these the possessions of a solitary emigré arriving in a new country after war? Are they the sacred relics of a healer, or the itemized exhibits used by a lawyer to incriminate an offender? Do they belong to a hoarder, a celebrity, a beggar, an alien, a survivor? Grow the character's story, using the first person to give voice to the objects and their significance. Write from each object's point of view. Then, using the third person, portray the character and objects from another character's point of view. What do we learn from the different perspectives?

13

NOTHING IS HOLDING YOU BACK

In 2010, PEN International marked the fiftieth year of its Writers in Prison Committee, one of the campaigning parts of this global organization dedicated to literature. For the anniversary, PEN published the life stories of 50 suppressed writers, each linked to a particular year.

I learned about Irina Ratushinskaya, a Ukrainian physicist and human rights activist, whose poems, distributed by the underground press, prompted imprisonment and a sentence of 12 years in a labour camp. Even when incarcerated, she continued to make poetry. How? She wrote verse on soap.

I read about the Vietnamese teacher Nguyễn Chí Thiện, who was charged with spreading 'anti-propaganda'. Despite repeated arrests and years of incarceration, he composed hundreds of poems, all of them committed to memory. Yes, he remembered them all, word for word, line for line. In a period of freedom, thinking he wouldn't survive another bout of jail, he braved the security police and gave his poetry – handwritten by this point – to British Embassy diplomats.

Writers in prison have to etch soap, commit to memory, scrawl with blood or juice on scraps or onion skins or toilet paper. Then, when they get out, when they can shout, they keep on writing – but often the authorities get them again, hacking at whatever is left of the person.

There are many writers, year by year, who are suppressed and silenced. We have the names of some, but how many are left unnamed, unheard, unsung? This is the most prolific author of all: *Anonymous*.

It's absurdly easy for me and you, with our liberty, our pens and paper, and technology aplenty. Nothing is holding us back. Let's treasure our freedom. Let's make the most of it. Let's write because we can.

14
WORD-WORLDS

In *A Midsummer Night's Dream*, Quince the carpenter exclaims at his newly metamorphosed friend: *Bless thee, Bottom! bless thee! thou art translated*. Translated? Yes, into a foreign language, a half-man-half-ass language. With an ass's head, Bottom suddenly likes eating dried peas, but he is also at the mercy of new asinine puns. His word-world has shifted.

Before the Norman Conquest of England in 1066, the locals could *shove* a *stool* up to a *bench* and *eat lamb*. Norman French did not replace English, but was added to it. After the conquerors had settled in, Anglo-Saxons could also *push* a *chair* towards a *table* and *dine* on *mutton*. The new words came with new concepts.

We say *la dolce vita* or *joie de vivre* or *schadenfreude* because there are no easy equivalents in English.

Indonesians speak only in the present tense, even when a story happened in the past. How immediate is that? Occasionally we do the same in English to bring history to life (*The year is 1564, and William Shakespeare is born…*), to relate personal anecdotes, and to tell jokes: *This guy walks into a bar and orders a double entendre. So the barman gives him one.*

Tibetans have no word for emotion, only a word that means negative, destructive emotion. I heard this from a Tibetan monk who was introduced as the incarnation of various historic yogis and tertons, an emanation of one of Buddha's heart-sons – and other fine descriptions besides. There are Tibetan words for a mountain of concepts that are virtually untranslatable.

Here's how one creative writing student transports his classmates to a new word-world, courtesy of an assignment I set: to describe a room from the point of view of an insect.

> *Eight legs moving together. Stop and move. Stop then eight legs move. Outside is wet and now must find dry, which is good. Find an opening, a small space and walk up, then over and then down a smooth surface. Legs stick to support descent. Stop and eyes sense. Much light. Light is bad. Good for enemies who eat eight legs. Need the dark to hide and wait. Wait for food.*
>
> *[...] After legs move many times, reach the hard sky where the three grounds meet. Good place to make web to bring food when the great fire disappears. Stop. Feel movement of air. Must be still. A giant four limb appears. Moves very fast and lies on giant sea of soft. Dark box in corner suddenly makes light and noise but no heat. Now dangerous, now must move.*

Everyone in the class listens very quietly as we become immersed in the spider's strange and solitary world. Nobody has any doubts about the room. We even agree on the physical dimensions of the space, no need for a single measurement. We fill in the gaps. We see the familiar – a ceiling, a television, carpet – in a totally unfamiliar way. We want to know more about the protagonist's intentions. What will eight legs do next? Where will eight legs take us?

The writer explains how he approached the brief. He didn't want to go the anthropomorphic route, the cunningly disguised human, even though this technique works a treat in *Animal Farm*, *The Wind in the Willows* and *Aesop's Fables*. He didn't want to describe, as Franz Kafka did, a conscious transition from human to insect. Having decided not to write another *Metamorphosis*, he found there were new questions to answer.

What makes a spider get up and go? Can a spider know itself? How does it perceive constructions like windows and walls? Other life forms? Spiders probably don't speak English (although you never know). To give a spider words, not to mention human notions of logic or narrative, is already inauthentic. But the line must be drawn somewhere, because all fiction is inauthentic.

The writer decides to draw the line as far from himself as he can, away from the conventions of his own perspective, without losing us in deepest spiderspace. Let's face it: he could have written *nh nh nh* until the ink ran out.

He makes his sentences uncharacteristically short and simple. Adjectives stand for nouns because sensations replace the things he, or we, would unthinkingly name. He disables his usual range of descriptive powers and develops a few select spidery ones. And he takes us with him.

Every language is a vision of the world, a way of seeing, not just a way of saying. You might be able to classify all the antiques in a room, you might feel comfortable analyzing a work of art, you might know at least ten grand words for a certain emotion, but if the character or voice in your work is very down-to-earth, you need to tailor your dictionary and your awareness to fit. This is an exercise in concentration and self-control, like giving yourself constraints in order to improve your creative stroke. It's also an exercise in empathy.

15
LET'S CROSS OVER

Get deep into fields and furrows with a peasant; now sit on an aristocrat's well-upholstered seat. Travel to the inner mind of the victim, then view it from the murderer's outpost. Settle down with people a thousand years ago. Start a new religion on an asteroid.

Writing is like travelling, only cheaper and with no border controls. When Jung Chang takes us into the China of *Wild Swans*, it is a geographical journey, to be sure. But it is also a psychological journey.

R.K. Narayan's *The Dark Room* is a retreat into depression, a place the abused protagonist learns to leave, if only to revisit. In *Giovanni's Room*, James Baldwin creates much more than a physical space – it's a place of profound transformation. A regular commuter train is a brave new world for the protagonist of *The Curious Incident of the Dog in the Night-Time*. A return to India is a return to childhood in Arundhati Roy's *The God of Small Things*.

When in Rome, Elizabeth Gilbert (*Eat, Pray, Love*) enjoyed saying *attraversiamo*. It simply means *let's cross*. You might say it to a friend when there's a gap in the traffic and it feels safe to make a dash across the road. But it took on greater dimensions for her, a psychological transition: *let's cross over.*

That's exactly what writing can be for you. A verbal crossing to the other side. The side where you do not fear death, perhaps. Or the side where you make sense of your upbringing. The side of your life that embraces love and vulnerability. The side of your culture you've wondered about but didn't have a good reason to visit. The side of your society that provokes strong feelings in you. Your confident side. Your funny side. The side of yourself you'd rather hide.

Attraversiamo.

16
WRITE WHAT YOU KNOW?

How can you write about dying if you haven't died yet? How can you write about the future? You know the dictum: *write what you know*. It's often flung at creative writing students and it's often misunderstood. A 'method' actor doesn't have to have killed people in order to understand a killer's point of view. A writer doesn't have to get pregnant in order to write about childbirth. Your own experience will inform your work but you don't have to be the perpetual protagonist.

What can you know?

Author Annie Proulx takes herself to new places, hunkers down, digs around, haunts little stores and buys heaps of second-hand books about farming, local history, auction records, hunting tackle, whatever. She transcribes wording from street signs and menus and advertising. She hangs about and absorbs conversations, noting the speech patterns, the vernacular, topics of concern. Soon enough, she knows the area. Narratives start to emerge. Stories take shape organically, almost as if they grow from the earth. This is how she does her research. She writes what she knows, but she didn't know it before she started delving.

If you research a mountain, you can write a molehill very well. You need to be able to choose freely, to make creative choices. What you leave out is as important as what you use. Your new-found knowledge may be interesting – it may even bring new joys into your life – but if you avoid plot-stopping-illusion-breaking-information-dumps, your readers will be happier too.

For each one of my books, fiction and non-fiction, I started out not knowing enough. I wrote about what I wanted to know – and (deep breath) I wrote about what I didn't know I wanted to know. Through writing, I came to know, and inhabit, and cherish new worlds.

Write to discover what you want to know.

Beyond knowing new worlds, there may be other rewards. It's pleasurable to question and explore. Scientific studies suggest that when we seek encounters with newness, our brains release dopamine and other 'feel-good' chemicals. Curiosity enhances positivity enhances curiosity.

17
RESEARCH IS A BEAUTIFUL PLACE

When I started working on a novel set in the USA, I knew that I was making all sorts of mistakes and assumptions. What did I know about American political history? Not enough. How could I set a story in America and get the language right, the nuances of different cultures and communities? I needed to do research.

After a period of deep immersion in books and websites (writing the fictional story all the while), I realized that I needed to go to Dallas, where JFK was assassinated, and to Detroit, where the motorcade limo is housed in a museum. I needed to interview assassinologists and religious fundamentalists.

Just as importantly, my fictional characters had already embarked on a fictional journey that required research of a non-touristy kind. I needed to drive from Dallas to Detroit, in a hurry, specifically avoiding the places that would feature in travel guides. It was to be a journey through anonymity. One of my protagonists thinks: 'There wasn't one single place along the route she'd ever heard of. Not even a real big city with a famous food. It was a road through nowhere.'

I wanted to see and feel the journey from my characters' perspectives. I needed the first-hand physical experience, the sensory stimulus of unfamiliar landscapes and weathers, the random motels, the feeling of highway food in my gut, an idea about local people and their ways of interacting, close-up views of remote places where poverty endures and the cameras don't come.

Without a specific story to tell, I might have taken such a trip just for the sake of it. But this wasn't a vague and absent-minded wandering. This was a focused, keenly observant journey. I made notes, took photos, collected ephemera. I had a purpose for being there. There was value in every detail that might make a difference for the story. Ordinary stuff. Daily life. Despite the lack of dramatic landmarks or world wonders, the trip was inspiring and I remember it vividly.

Ordinary or extraordinary, such experiences are powerful because you're not just an onlooker or a passer-by. You have the confidence to talk to strangers, letting them know that you're researching and writing, inviting them to share their world with you. People usually appreciate being valued, being heard. These personal connections enrich your life experience, your understanding of others, your imagination, your empathy – not just your literary work.

If you're writing about a murder, you might need to get inside a courthouse and a prison, you might need to hold a real weapon, you might need to interview a pathologist, a forensic psychiatrist, a bereaved person, a murderer, a mortician. As a writer, you can choose to go to places you would never get to otherwise, and have experiences of a rare and amazing kind.

Are you a researcher who writes, or a writer who researches? It doesn't matter if you marry your desire to know with your desire to create.

Research can become a fancy version of other writing-avoidance activities, such as dish washing or dog walking. If you let this tendency go unchecked, you'll find yourself sitting on a heap of research, which is fine if you want to sit on a heap of research, but not fine if you want to write a story.

Let your writing develop hand-in-hand with research. A bit of output, a bit of input. Even if it means feeling your way into the story for a while, and stumbling here and there, you'll be able to return to your first workings and correct, refine or add details.

You might feel daunted by the prospect of research, realizing how little you know of the world you want to write about. You might feel tempted to give up before you get properly started.

My advice? Don't let your lack of knowledge deter you from writing about anything. At all. Approach your subject matter with respect. Read and browse. Depending on your story's setting, you might need to travel, but your journeys needn't be long-haul. Seek out the experts to interview – the metallurgist, the mycologist, the firefighter, the war vet, the shipping enthusiast – whatever expertise your story needs. Don't be discouraged by the ones who say no. The ones who say yes will share real-life knowledge with you. Their insights and anecdotes are likely to inspire you in ways you couldn't imagine when you were planning your questions, and they might lead your writing in exciting new directions. Reassuringly, these people might also be amenable to checking the relevant parts of your work once it's written.

Research is an intensely, infinitely beautiful place, and it's easier to get to than you think.

Once you're there, you'll encounter communities of interesting people who'll be willing to connect with you. You're likely to discover fascinating detail and difference, as well as feelings of common humanity.

18
SPEND, SPEND, SPEND

Words don't cost a penny. They're not just affordable or cheap, they're free.

You can abuse words and they won't fight back. You can give three full-time jobs to one single word and it won't complain or quit. Poets are notorious for this kind of verbal exploitation. Words will tell you secrets about yourself that you didn't know – without charging for the service as psychics and psychiatrists do. Words will catch you unawares and make you laugh. They will make you feel as proud as any doting parent, without the financial sacrifices, although I make no promises about sleepless nights.

You can endlessly reorganize words into different sequences. You can play with words and they will play with you as if you are their very best friend, which is handy when you've become a hermit and/or writer – that is, solitary.

In Shakespeare's drama *Richard II*, the true pain of exile is being shunned from

> *The language I have learn'd these forty years,*
> *My native English...*

Never mind real humans! You can hear the writer's own panic here, as his banished character imagines the horror of losing his linguistic identity forever. Banishment from England means 'speechless death'. Lose words and you lose all of society.

The deposed king tries to populate his dungeon with verbal subjects:

> *I have been studying how I may compare*
> *This prison where I live unto the world:*
> *And, for because the world is populous,*
> *And here is not a creature but myself,*
> *I cannot do it; – yet I'll hammer't out.*

Yet he'll hammer it out? That's the writer talking, not the ruler. He's determined to make that metaphor work, despite its doubtful potential. It pays off. Richard fills his cell with words. If it weren't for the assassins who come to silence him forever, he would carry on playing with words ad infinitum.

There's a lesson here for all of us. Even if your first words feel misspent or profligate, keep spending. Be extravagant. Revel and squander. The more words you use, the more you seem to have. They're a guilt-free, limitless resource. Let yourself play with joyful abandon. Live it up.

Your purpose? Pointless fun.

You don't need scientists to tell you how invaluable this can be for your vitality and productivity.

19
DREAM BIG

If you want to create a fire in a film, or a scary monster, you have to think carefully about the practicalities: insurance, pyrotechnics, special effects, egos… The budget gets ridiculous. Will a phone call about a fire do? Maybe a monster can be heard and not seen? You need to bend the story and trim the script.

Think how easy it is to summon up a monster in a poem or piece of prose. You just say the word. No elaborate prosthetics, no costly CGI, not even a cut-price armourer to ensure the health and safety of cast and crew in the presence of fire and/or scary monsters.

Blow the budget, because there is none. Expansive is not expensive. Be lavish with your imagination. Dream big, dream far, dream impossible, dream beyond.

20
NOTHING IS WASTED

William Golding's published novel *Lord of the Flies* begins with Ralph and another stranded schoolboy meeting by a lagoon. They're already on the island. Poor Piggy reveals his nickname…

But Golding's handwritten draft began with pages and pages of carefully written prose about a plane 'packed with a job lot of children' in the midst of an atomic war, an attack, a crash – and *then* the island. That contextual narrative was discarded in favour of a more dramatic first chapter, although its logic remains implicit in the final story.

The discarded words were not wasted.

Creative writing is an iterative process. Sometimes you need to write A and B in order to get to C – which is actually, unexpectedly, the start – whereupon you can go back and trash A and B. Occasionally, you'll reach the real heart of your poem or story halfway through. That's when you must be bold and fill the bin. Don't think of the discards as a waste of time or brain. You needed them to lead you, word by word, idea by idea, to the true beginning.

I'm shy of trashing, so I set up a folder for scraps. It is constantly active, with stuff going in: paragraphs I've slaved over, phrases I cling to for their darling beauty, detailed chapters I've polished obsessively before moving on with the plot. Entire characters lie at rest in my scrap folder, forever ready to be raised from the dead. But guess what? I never go back to retrieve what I've thrown away.

A good writer-friend read an early draft of my last novel and said it felt like two novels. Too many perspectives. Too many locations. Too many years.

The book needed major surgery, but I felt attached to the artefact I'd created. I knew I needed cool distance and clarity of thought. So I let it be for a while. Then I printed the whole thing out and did my best to withdraw from the real world, reading the 'big picture' of the text rather than getting caught up in small details. I was a hermit for a week. I tried to keep my mind clutter-free. I could see that I needed to throw away about a third of my book. I lopped off the beginning (a few thousand words). I lopped off the end – about 30,000 painstakingly researched, written and edited words. The remaining body of text needed work to create structural balance. It needed more research. And more words. They came more easily than I expected. It was as if they'd been waiting there all along.

Once I'd done with all that 'surgery', a less brutal image settled in my mind.

I thought about how a rainforest evolves. Certain plants can appear only after other plants have flourished, done their job and died. The growth of different plants, different storeys, is sequential, consequential.

Nothing is wasted.

Stinging brush plants, pioneer words, false starts, warm-ups, drafts, darlings… Let them happen. Let them create the nourishing mulch, the shade, the right conditions for the next generation to germinate and come into being.

I'm referring to writing, of course, but it begins to feel like an idea for living.

21
ALL YOU NEED IS...

There are many arts that begin with just a few basics: all you need is your body to move… found objects to arrange or embellish, to blow or beat… something to make marks… But the props and tools of writing stay basic, even if you're writing *War and Peace*. Writing is so low-tech it's almost not an art.

You don't need performance spaces or spectators. You don't need a kiln, forge, workshop, artisan community, elaborate software/hardware. There's no call for precious pigments, or archival paper cold-pressed by water nymphs. You don't need instruments made of linden wood or intestines. You can live without fancy tech and glorious acoustics. You don't even need noise-tolerant neighbours; the practice of writing is mostly inaudible.

The only workforce you need is you.

The only technology you need is a writing implement (a digital device is nice, but a quill will do) and a surface on which to write.

Mobilize that workforce and utilize that technology, regularly, creatively, attentively.

Enough is all you need.

22
POSSIBLY YOUR GREATEST TALENT

You've heard the old joke. One guy says: 'I'm writing a book.' The other guy replies: 'Really? Neither am I.'

Procrastination is the greatest creative talent of every writer. The ideas unleashed by procrastination are infinite, as many as there are grains of sand in all the deserts, as many as there are drops of water in all the oceans.

Wait for the perfect moment, the overview, the clear schedule, the neat room, the right pyjamas, the noble muse and the page/screen will remain blank.

Micro-procrastination

The dishes need doing. The friends need seeing. The widgets need sorting. I must get a haircut. Just look at those weeds. One website leads to another.

Work, mood, friends, family, fear of failure – life and all its excuses get in the way. Acknowledge the talent you have for procrastination and never again say you're not good at anything. You are a champion of procrastination, the record-breaking hero of avoidance, a demi-god of delay. Honour your talent.

Then conceal it, even from yourself, like those martial arts masters who conquer all enemies because they hide their mastery and they hide their intent.

Macro-procrastination

Some people say that their retirement dream is 'finally to write that book'. This is existential procrastination, a grander form than the daily widget-sorting variety.

To such people I say: 'Why wait until then? What's keeping you from doing it now?'

You have the means, the motive and the opportunity.
(But it's not a crime.)

You don't need expensive resources.
(One writing implement. One surface.)

You can always make time.
(Less bed-time, less browse-time, less TV-time…)

You want to do it.
(Indulge your fantasy.)

And you are alive now.
(Death will happen.)

Don't put off until tomorrow what you can write today.
All you need is to do it. Today.

23
PUT OFF PROCRASTINATION

If procrastination is emanating from your every pore, some of the remedies here may be effective for you. But discontinue at the first sign of unwelcome side-effects, such as Writer's Block.

Join a class

Whether it's a degree or a short course, the idea is to practise your craft with the guidance of a skilled writer-teacher and the wisdom of a peer group. You will learn from doing, and from what other people do. You'll hear when writing is effective, or not. You'll hear how others solve creative problems and respond to your work. If you turn up, attempt the assigned tasks and join in discussion, you will boost your skills and confidence. Fixed programmes and homework are invaluable for the solitary procrastinator – er, writer.

Set up a writing routine

Create a time when you know you will write. It can be a matter of hours, or days, each week. It needs to be regular. A habit. A rhythm. It's important to mark this commitment in your diary. Nothing else can be booked into this spot. Give it importance and let others know that this time is blocked out. You'll see that your ideas start gathering and, when you sit down to write, you'll be ready. If words don't flow at first, resist the temptation to do anything else. Allow yourself time to sit and think.

Press pause

[PAUSE] Practise a focusing activity, such as meditation, yoga, tai chi, swimming, running or walking. [PAUSE] Find a place where you know you can write, ideally unsociable and distraction-free, perhaps the local library, a café, or a corner at home that you can make your own. One writer I know puts on headphones and a specific soundtrack to get into the writing zone anytime, anywhere. [PAUSE] Go away for a writing retreat, communal or solitary, somewhere serene and safe. [PAUSE] Turn off all tech, especially mail and social media. Or, if you have the willpower of a gnat, turn on the tech designed to block the tech: dedicated anti-distraction software. I know of one journalist who stows his internet router in a time-lock safe. [PAUSE] Wear ear-plugs, blinkers and a *Do Not Disturb* sign – if you're into that sort of thing. [PAUSE]

Give yourself a deadline

Since creativity feels erratic or ethereal, it can help to pin it down with times and dates. Specific deliverables may be useful too. You can make a deadline more concrete if you promise to deliver the work to someone else, but maybe it's enough to make the promise to yourself. Try one of these: *I'll start writing at this hour every day. I'll do this number of words (or pages) each week. I'll finish the first draft before my next birthday. I'll enter this poetry competition. I'll submit my non-fiction book proposal before spring.* On the other hand, there is the Douglas Adams approach, where the appeal of deadlines is the sound-effect they produce. As they fly past.

Get a writing buddy

You know how a buddy can help with getting fit or quitting a bad habit: you make the effort because the other person makes the effort. Just when they feel ready to surrender, you spur them on. At the moment when you're ready to give up or give in, they are your conscience. You can't let them down. Get a writing buddy who's as serious about writing as you are. Agree your terms and conditions. Stick to the plan.

Make a circle

Writing groups come in all shapes and sizes. Online and offline. In pubs, cafés, hotel lobbies, people's homes. Some groups are devoted to one kind of work, say, playwriting, while others are agnostic about form or genre. There are meet-ups run by characterful leaders, and others that are leaderless. I'm in a group that gets together after work once a week. We each read an extract of prose in progress, or we brainstorm ideas. I know another writing group that meets once a month and devotes a full day to one writer's work, thoroughly read and marked up beforehand. Find the writing group that suits you. Or start one of your own. *(There's more about this in Chapter 96.)*

24
THE CLOAK OF INVISIBILITY

Are you worried about putting your work out there? Do you hate being the centre of attention? Perhaps you're camera-shy, or just… shy. One writer I know, who is provocative in his fiction, boldly comical, almost an exhibitionist, mumbles and hunches in real life. Many writers prefer to wander lonely as a cloud, or skulk about in a garret, rather than stand in the glare of a spotlight.

Not every writer is a performing pony on the literary festival circuit. And even when they are, people gather to experience the brain at work, not the brawn or beauty. If writers achieve fame or notoriety, they can walk down a busy city street and not be assaulted by fans or paparazzi. Close your eyes. How much easier is it to picture Hannibal Lecter than Thomas Harris?

History is littered with writerly cloaks of invisibility. Jane Austen never saw her own name printed on her books. Mary Ann Evans knew that she needed to be a man to get her fiction published and taken seriously, so she called herself George Eliot. Bestselling writer Dick Francis turns out to be not one, but two: a husband-and-wife team. In interviews, he referred to himself as Richard, and his wife as Mary, explaining that the author known as 'Dick Francis' was both of them together. As for *My Brilliant Friend* author 'Elena Ferrante', she made an existential choice from the outset of her writing career: absolute anonymity.

There's another cloak of invisibility you can wear. It's the day-job.

One friend of mine is a poet, but he works full-time as a painter and decorator, and has done so ever since he left school. He thinks about his subjects and his words as he fills, sands, papers, paints, washes brushes. He writes after-hours, but he always has a notebook in his pocket.

It's unlikely that you've heard of my painter-decorator friend by name, even though his poetry has been published. But you have probably heard of insurance executive Wallace Stevens, the lawyer and insurance company employee Franz Kafka, and Anton Chekhov, who was a physician and considered that to be his main profession.

Even in this era of celebrity and social media, the cloak of invisibility is a timeless classic any writer can wear. Don't worry if you're shy and retiring. Introversion can be conducive to inventiveness, and solitude can help with focus. When the world seems to be promoting noise and speed, honour your quiet power. You can be patient, you can be shy. Just don't be shy of writing.

25
IT DOESN'T MATTER A JOT

Books gather dust and take up space. Your voice is one of many. The world is not holding its breath waiting for your poetry. The planet's problems will not be fixed by your play. Your writing work is not a matter of life and death, unlike the work of a surgeon, firefighter or soldier. Even if you write the greatest story ever told, it's possible that nobody will read it, let alone pay actual money for it. Write 20 books, and so what.

Nobody really cares.

Is this disheartening? No, it's liberating.

Now you are free to enjoy the journey. The exploration. The discipline. The perspiration. The progress. The angst. The failure. The focus. The insight. The obsession. The frustration. The magic moments. The tinkering. The discovery. The solitude. The inspiration. The graft. The purpose. The bliss. The perseverance. The attention to that pesky, puny detail immaterial to all but you. The sense of completion. The sense of incompletion.

Your artefact, your 'it', doesn't matter.

Is this dispiriting? No, it's exhilarating.

26
IT MATTERS
A WHOLE LOT

A writer-friend of mine says that to create or find meaning, some people have religion, some people have children. She herself doesn't have religion, and she doesn't have children.

'I write.' She says it with a full stop. 'I'm not saying that it brings meaning. But I don't know what I'd do without it.'

Like her, I feel unmoored when I'm not writing. Incomplete. Not quite myself.

Maybe this is a way of saying that writing is addictive. And yet, unlike other addictions, the effects of writing are likely to be beneficial. Apart from the chronic condition of Writer's Rump,* writing is positively healthful. Writing as self-expression – therapeutic or artistic or both – can help build the practitioner's resilience.

Beyond the world of the self, writing matters a whole lot in the wider world.

We can read and write stories that bring us closer to our fellow human beings. To see inside a different culture is to de-otherize, to humanize. Once you see the world from another person's point of view, you're less likely to harm them. This is a path to understanding and compassion, which is surely also a path to peace.

Visual artist Marlene Dumas writes beautifully about this, suggesting that entire generations within military cultures can end up 'thinking only in enemy-images'. Art, she proposes, 'is a way of sleeping with the enemy.'

Write your path to peace. It matters.

✱ *Writer's Rump:* an inflammation of the posterior induced by sitting lonely as a cloud for long periods of time, which condition is adversely affected by poor circulation. Hence *Writer's Block* (cf. *Housemaid's Knee, Policeman's Heel*).

27
READING LOVES WRITING LOVES READING

In earlier centuries, aspiring visual artists were taught to copy the 'masters'. The trainee patiently worked in the school of, or in the style of, the artist they most admired. Brushstroke by brushstroke. Hair wisp by hair wisp. Gleam by gleam. This practice increased the scale and scope of an established artist's business, while giving employment to unknown beginners. Most importantly, it gave the apprentices insight into technique, theory, expertise – and insight into their own competence. But not all learners are happy simply repeating directives. Individuality will out. History is peppered with apprentices who became masters in their own right, having absorbed, accepted or rejected what they were taught, before lighting on their own unique approach.

Speaking a language (your own or another) comes so much more easily when you're surrounded by it, hearing it flexed and probed by others. The same goes for writing. Read, and you'll immerse yourself in the world of words, you'll be absorbing and taking apart everything from syntax and structure to ideology and ideas.

Read as much as you can, observing how a writer does or doesn't succeed in creating a certain emotional effect, argument or narrative arc. Copy long passages from books you like, authors you like – this is a good way to get inside the craft. But do this by handwriting, as it slows you down enough to lay the craft bare and give you time to think. For a while, you might slip into writing just like your hero. That's fine. It's normal. And you'll get over it. William Faulkner's first published works are described as Joycean because he wrote in awe of James Joyce, but he soon got past the imitative stage and found his own sound and fury.

Reading is good for your writing because a writer has to be smart at acquiring knowledge, smart at interpreting, and smart at telling or retelling. But don't take it from me. In an influential paper called *What Reading Does for the Mind*, professors Anne E. Cunningham and Keith E. Stanovich concluded after years of intensive research that 'ability is not the only variable that counts in the development of intellectual functioning. Those who read a lot will enhance their verbal intelligence; that is, reading will make them smarter.'

If that isn't enough academic ballast for all writer-readers, I'll quote novelist and playwright Carl Djerassi, one of the chemists behind the invention of the synthetic contraceptive pill. I went to a talk at the British Library where he said, quite simply, 'you can only be a writer if you read.'

Over to you, dear Reader. You know what to do.

28
THE PERFECT SPONGE

Look up the definition of *sponge*. It's a well-loaded word.

> An animal without a backbone, usually hollow, hermaphroditic, soft and sessile.

> A porous material.

> A heavy drinker.

> Someone who soaks up the generosity of others.

> A kind of cake.

Apart from the cake, most writers are all of these.

So, how to make the perfect sponge? Well, reading is a very good start. Read as much as you can, absorbing as much as you can, because reading loves writing. But you need to soak up more than words. Be receptive, be impressionable. Attract. Gather. Make your entire self into one thirsty, capacious, porous entity.

Cultural input of all kinds expands the sponge. See films, discuss them.

Go to the theatre. Analyze dance. Make a date with a museum. Attend festivals and readings and talks. Listen to writers in interview. Visit inspiring places. Visit dull places. Do research. Keep a notebook. Do classes. Do more classes.

OK, that's the secondary stuff.

Then there's the primary stuff. Life. Learn from the hundreds of people who intersect your life in tiny and not-so-tiny ways. You're not nearly so interesting as they are. What's their story? Why do they get so excited about football or neighbours or limpets? Don't tell them what you know about these things; allow space for what they know. Drink in their words. Absorb their gestures and expressions. Take in their reasoning. See things – the terrain, the crisis, the limpet, the cake – from their point of view.

Friedrich Nietzsche had similar suggestions for becoming a good novelist. He called it a recipe, and I'm wondering if he, too, was thinking about cake. Here's a taste:

> *Do not talk about giftedness, inborn talents! [...] One should be tireless in collecting and describing human types and characters; one should above all relate things to others and listen to others relate, keeping one's eyes and ears open for the effect produced on those present, one should travel like a landscape painter or costume designer; [...] one should, finally, reflect on the motives of human actions, disdain no signpost for instruction about them and be a collector of these things day and night.*

Be a collector of these things day and night.

29

CRAFT IS SOMETHING YOU CAN LEARN

'But can creative writing be taught?'

Many people ask me this, dubiously, eyebrows knitting, certain of the impossibility. Their assumption is that talent, imagination and wordsmithery cannot be learned, that you've either got it or you ain't.

I don't assume this.

Writing is a craft. Like mask-making. Pottery. Woodworking. It is something you can learn. Don't let anyone persuade you otherwise.

In class I always stress the craft of writing (as opposed to, say, the commercial side). I can't teach someone talent or imagination, but I can try to nurture both. Sometimes they have been suppressed by habit, work or fear of failure.

My repeated refrain is that the more you practise any craft, the better you get at it. Creative writing classes are a great start, but you need to continue with practice on your own. This practice involves thinking, writing, editing, reading – and persevering.

Craft learning doesn't always happen in neatly progressive stages. You can feel brilliantly competent one week, struggling the next. This might have as much to do with your mood as anything else. You need to learn to write through inspirations and blocks with such craft that the artefact is not scarred by your highs and lows. You might find that a certain aspect of writing (say, dialogue) glitters as it flows. Moments later, you might be struggling with a tiny plot point. But with craft you can make it all connect and cohere.

There are no right or wrong answers, no mathematical proofs or certainties. There are no last words on what is good or bad, although opinions can be more or less informed. The point is, the more you do it, the better you'll get at it.

Try writing something every day.

If it helps, think of these four Ps as a motto.

> Practice.
>
> Patience.
>
> Persistence.
>
> Progress.

30
PERFECT IS THE ENEMY OF GOOD

We literary types can be sensitive and aspiring and insecure all at once, so we can let the blank page defeat us with its perfection. Non-doing seems safer than doing. We worry that what we write won't be good enough. That it's not original. That it creaks and leaks. That other people won't want to read it.

So be it.

Writing exercises are good for you because they don't matter.
You are free to practise and play.

Here are some thoughts to help you resist the cunning and destructive Enemy of Good:

1. Don't fear making a mistake. Make lots of mistakes.

2. Aim for adequate. Good enough is enough.

3. An instrument will teach you what you need to know to play it.

4. If you can't decide whether to go wild or behave, go wild.

5. Too much control and you have a dissertation, not a creative work.

6. If you come to a crossroads and you don't know what to do, it's better to go along a road, even if it's the wrong one, rather than stand still.

7. Get the bad version out of your system.

8. You are not Shakespeare. Nor is anyone else.

9. The moment you say 'I don't care what others think' is the moment you liberate your creative self.

10. The more you write, the more you'll write well.

Try this joyful exercise: write rubbish. Write as much rubbish as you like. Keep writing rubbish until you run out of words/rubbish.

31
PERFECT IS
THE ENEMY OF
INTERESTING

Naive art, low-budget films, fan fiction... Many artworks that are deemed imperfect by academy standards inspire fierce love and loyalty. Why? They dislodge us from our usual orbits. They touch us with sincerity of feeling. They draw us into their worldview.

What do you prefer: a few sublime ideas in an unruly book, or a well-constructed work that follows all the rules? 'Perfect' works of art often leave me cold. They tick all the boxes. They're well-behaved. The producers and the promoters are happy. But everything is so polished and proud that I feel shut out. I'd much rather a flawed, brave, independent work that dares to take heartfelt risks.

Mozart wrote about some of his own concertos that they were brilliant and held the happy balance between being too difficult and too easy – but he was concerned that they missed *poverty.*

I'm intrigued by this idea of poverty, this sense of lack or deficiency.

I think it's another way of saying *vulnerability*.

The not-perfect.

If writing is uniform, too complete, too comfortable, too slick or smooth, we slip off – which is the opposite of being engaged.

Write with poverty. Embrace your vulnerability. Let people in.

32
EVERYONE IS EQUAL

Writers are nothing if not beginners. That goes for all of us, whether we're writing our very first screenplay or hundredth poem.

My tai chi teacher likes to say: *Zen mind, beginner's mind.* It's a state of mind that we seek to attain. A kind of innocence in the depth of experience. An approach that is open-minded and open-hearted.

Degree courses offer structure through modules and marks, but creative capability is not measurable in neat stages. When you apply yourself to any artistic activity, it's helpful to think about progress, not perfection. You may have accumulated some life experience, and you may have devoted 10,000 hours to the craft of writing, but each time you *create* you are making something new – which means that you are a perpetual beginner.

There are no black belts. No military ranks or pay grades. Enjoy life without distances, speeds or levels to attain. Relish being at the start of something new, alongside every other writer.

33
CREATING
TIME AND SPACE

Your first creative act? Make time and space.

TIME

A regular time. Enough time, with pondering time.

SPACE

A comfortable place. A play space. Your own spot.

TIME + SPACE = POSITIVE WRITING POWER

HAPPY
MIDDLES

Happy Middles are about complication in the most positive sense: being under way, paying attention, fuelling up, developing the craft, fine-tuning skills, cultivating discipline, appreciating life. Dive in here for how-to guidance, some literal, some lateral.

34
THE LEAP
OF FAILURE

Any creative endeavour opens you up to the possibility of failure. If you pursue a creative life every day, you face failure every day. Again and again throughout the day. It's a precipice.

People doing other work may feel this too. As a parent, as a miner, as an administrator, as anything in this world, there is the possibility of failure at every turn. We all make mistakes.

But there is something spectacular about the way creativity sets you up to fail. There's no communal safety-net for the shock of the new: others may respond to your work with admiration, ridicule or indifference. If you *don't* brave something new, your work may be dismissed as formulaic or dull. The wisdom here is not to get too caught up in what others think.

If you are in fact creating, you are making something that has not been made before, not even by you. It's trial and error. And error. Become a creative writer, and fear of failure is part of your identity. So what? You'll survive. It's not like failing while performing brain surgery – a dead patient matters more than your misunderstood artwork.

Be open to failure. Loosen up. Feel your fear. Observe it. Expose your soul. Toughen up. Learn. Take the approach Thomas Edison took: each unsuccessful attempt at designing a light bulb was not a *failure*, but a *step to success*.

Failure makes you a better maker.

Accepting failure, learning from it, makes you a better person.

If failure is a precipice, you can stumble over it, or you can jump with your best wings on.

35
LOVE YOUR NOTEBOOK

Just as visual artists fill sketchbooks with drawings and ideas, writers fill notebooks. I have boxes full of notebooks, the sort that match, travel and stack easily. I have scrapbook files on my laptop. And a few thousand individual notes keyed into my smartphone. Oh, and voice memos too.

This is a messy habit. I urge you to try it.

Start a notebook. Papery or digital or both. Keep it active. Fill it with scraps and titbits. Keep it on you at all times – except when bathing. Don't use it for admin or chores.

Have it ready for the dialogue you overhear by chance, the moment you misread a sign, the brainwave that happens just before sleep, the dream you wake up remembering, the scene you witness on the way to work, the intriguing fact you remember or discover, the thoughts you have after seeing a film or hearing the news, the image of someone you happen to notice, the spontaneous reminiscences of an older person, the new experiences you have when you travel, the accidental collision of three words that strike you, randomly, as beautiful.

Don't worry about anyone reading your notebook. It's for your eyes only. It's a repository of prompts, seemingly useless, potentially of mysterious value. One day, when you're suffering from Writer's Block, you might flick through your jottings and light upon inspiration in the margins. Years from now, you might be able to point to a hasty old notelet that grew into your groundbreaking drama. The very act of writing, even in a rushed scribble, helps you to think, verbalize and remember ideas.

Beyond aesthetic fitness, there are other psychological rewards. In her essay 'On Keeping a Notebook', author Joan Didion writes that 'we are talking about something private, about bits of the mind's string too short to use, an indiscriminate and erratic assemblage with meaning only for its maker.'

I love those random bits of mental string.

Didion continues with an even more emotive point about remembering and our sense of selfhood, saying that 'we forget all too soon the things we thought we could never forget. We forget the loves and the betrayals alike, forget what we whispered and what we screamed, forget who we were.'

Our scrawls and sketches connect us powerfully with our former selves.

36
KEEP A DIARY

Your diary is a storehouse for the uncensored, unstructured, primary material of your daily life, your dreams, travels, childhood memories, passions, concerns, your unedited thoughts about work, family and friends. You don't have to worry about the audience because the audience is just you (unless you have other purposes in mind).

Keeping a journal is a way of maintaining writing-muscle fitness, making sense of the chaos of experience, and enjoying therapeutic release, like chatting to a trusted intimate without self-consciousness or fear. Your diary keeps your secrets.

Don't attempt to write out your entire day, every day. A map with a scale of 1:1 is no map. You could choose a theme, just one strand of experience – say, the music you've been listening to, where and how you hear it, what effects it has on you. Or you could focus on the places you've been to, physically and imaginatively, and see what thoughts take shape in your writing.

If you do only one thing in the diary department, I urge you to try your hand at this: gratitude. Make a regular record of the day's blessings: a pleasurable experience, a kind gesture, an accomplishment, a loved one, a smile, a gift, a moment of beauty. They needn't be colossal or numerous.

Positive journalling is not to avoid or deny negative experiences with 'positive thinking'. It's not about papering over cracks. It's about taking a few minutes to remember and focus on the not-cracks. Your happy notes have neurochemical effects. Write before going to sleep at night, drift off with a smile in your mind, and your dormant body will be suffused with benevolence.

Studies show that, over time, this positive writing ritual can lower stress and anxiety levels, while boosting self-confidence, clarity of thought and resilience. In other words, you could be writing yourself happy.

37
ETHICAL EAVESDROPPING

'Joe! What a surprise! How the hell are you?'

'I'm good... pretty good...'

'Come in... sit down... what a surprise. When did you get back? Why didn't you let me know?'

'Wow! This place looks great.'

—I have to interrupt. Interesting how the first guy asks why Joe didn't let him know he was coming back. I suspect there's a hint of trouble in that question, but I may be wrong. Joe adds to my disquiet when he doesn't answer the question. Why doesn't he answer? Why didn't he let his friend know? And who cares if the place looks great? Actually, it matters, we realize, as the conversation continues without the help of authorial prose between the utterances.

The complete dialogue scene is read out in class. The following week, this student-writer tackles the same scene with descriptive prose narrated in the third person and set in the past. She likes it better because it answers her own questions about the characters' motivations. She is able to fly back to an earlier past, to explain unsaid thoughts and feelings, to fill in the gaps by telling us more than the spoken words would allow.

But in class we all like the dialogue scene much more. We've enjoyed the illusion of looking directly into other people's lives, 'eavesdropping' rather than reading a mediated report. Our curiosity is piqued by what's not said. The joy of interpretation has been left to us. We want to know and read more.

In some situations, listening secretly to others without their consent can be unethical. But in the world of creative writing – fiction, non-fiction, drama and poetry – two kinds of eavesdropping are not only ethical, I'd say they're vital.

1. The illusion of eavesdropping is a desirable effect created by the writer through well-crafted dialogue.

2. The practice of eavesdropping is a duty of the writer in public places.

Listen to the chatter of strangers on a train. Make notes from the shouted phone monologue you hear on the street. Pay attention to the tics of speech and regional quirks of your co-worker's banter. Write down the phrases that fly off the tongue of a specialist – the architect who refers to a timber spoon rather than a wooden spoon, the civil servant who talks of running a deficit but really means he's broke. Notice the distinctive vocabulary and syntax of people you encounter, a child, an elderly person, a sports coach, a market stallholder, an electronics salesman.

Your notes are verbal sketches. You have no idea yet what will become of them. Perhaps nothing more than the honing of your perceptual powers. Perhaps a new character, or the start of a poem. Perhaps a greater attunement to the thoughts and feelings of different people – which is not only ethical, it's a step towards the golden rule of treating others as you'd wish to be treated yourself.

38
SMELL BETTER

How often has a scent recalled for you, in an instant, a childhood experience, or a state of mind, or a significant person? Smell is a precious portal to involuntary memory.

The animal inside all of us knows that a bad odour is a warning – that food may be rotten, that water may be poisonous, that death or disease lurk nearby. Retailers know to exploit the emotive effects of smell, releasing scents to draw us in and keep us shopping. Property agents advise clients to brew fresh coffee when they're selling their homes; the aroma makes prospective buyers feel warm and comfortable.

In film and TV drama, smell is evoked by showing. A sickened detective covers his nose with a handkerchief when the victim's body is revealed. A mother nuzzles her baby's clothes. A lost traveller catches a hopeful whiff of a camp-fire on the wind. Any story does well to summon up smell.

There are two novels every writer should read to develop nose-power: *Perfume* by Patrick Süskind and *Jitterbug Perfume* by Tom Robbins.

After reading *Perfume*, I was obsessed for weeks, months, with how the world smelled. I became aware of every wispy waft that wandered into my nostrils, and every common-or-garden scent, not to mention the strident stinks that would always demand attention. It was as if my physical environment had become more porous, a flowing in and out of inhalations and exhalations, rather than an arrangement of discrete concrete objects. This is nothing if not alchemy: words become smells become a new world.

What of this newly aromatic universe?

For the reader, it's a fresh experience gained from literature, a kind of travelling to another perceptual place. Long after reading the fragrant fiction of Süskind and Robbins, the extra dimension to my perceptions has remained.

For the writer, there's a hefty clue here. You don't have to be creating a story about perfume to make good use of it. Think of the vividly sensory prose in Arundhati Roy's novel *The God of Small Things*.

Describe, evoke, provoke, using the power of smell to tell. Lay aside your visual tools for a while, and use your olfactory kit. Yes, we are interested in how a character looks – but how do they smell? This strong emotional information will tell us plenty about the smeller and the smellee too. Yes, we want to visualize a place, but its scent can suck us in, and linger longer in our memory. Redolent reading is more immersive.

If you smell more effectively, you'll write more effectively.

You can build your olfactory fitness through regular exercise. Act like a curious dog crossed with a serious wine expert. Close your eyes in order to analyze aromas – not just those of pretty flowers or appetizing food; inhale and appreciate the stinks too. Fill your notebook with verbal smell sketches. Delight in the working life of your particular peculiar nose. It'll be an expansion of your engagement with the world. A kind of mindfulness. Nosefulness?

39
WAKE UP AND HEAR THE COFFEE

Here are some of my notes about a courtyard in Venice: *Leafy vines and creepers veiling tall stone walls. Glimpses of old terracotta rooftops beyond. Soft slanting sunlight. Birds swooping down for crumbs. The aromas of coffee and baking. Expert waiters to and fro, serving tourists idling at wrought-iron tables.*

But this recollection is incomplete because the sound has been turned off. Distinct from the hush of conversation – voices, accents, languages – there were the songbirds, busy and excitable with spring, twittering. There were doves and pigeons, purring, purring. One of the waiters whistled as he worked: Venetian tunes, Frank Sinatra, opera. From a nearby campanile, church bells clanged, loud and deep and slow and irregular. Dimmed by distance, other bells thudded and donged. Sudden bells from another, closer church tumbled in, cascading from high to low notes, repeating, dwindling, until only the aftersound lingered, almost audible, almost an imaginary bell-breath.

In Wallace Stevens' poem 'Thirteen Ways of Looking at a Blackbird', the following stanza, one of thirteen ways of looking, is actually about thinking and listening:

> *I do not know which to prefer,*
> *The beauty of inflections*
> *Or the beauty of innuendoes,*
> *The blackbird whistling*
> *Or just after.*

Sounds, and their aftersounds, are as evocative as smells. But what do they evoke? Memory, emotion, a strong sense of place.

Think how irresistible a stray song can be, the way it reaches your ears through the muddle of noise in a public space: you are taken, almost bodily, into another context, another time.

And think about the influence of sound design in cinema. Alfred Hitchcock said that 33 percent of the effect of *Psycho* was due to the music. He was talking about Bernard Herrmann's alarming score. It is said that *Psycho* was passed by censors – after earlier rejection – only because the famous shower scene was temporarily stripped of its music. As I write, I can hear those shocking, stabbing, screeching sounds.

Don't forget the influence of sound in writing.

Think of yourself as composer and conductor too. Summon up a soundtrack to be heard in your reader's mind. You don't need years of musicology, you just need to hear, in your mind's ear. Think of yourself as a Foley artist crunching on gravel or slamming doors. Be an aural designer, releasing sound effects from your infinite catalogue of squeaks, squelches, swishes, tinkles, crackles, rumbles, hums, thuds, throbs, growls…

If you listen more effectively, you'll write more effectively. You'll hear the rhythms of sentences, you'll hear the tones and cadences of spoken words, and you'll be better able to fine-tune it all.

Auditory skills can be enhanced through regular training – a kind of earful meditation. Set a timer for five minutes. Close your eyes and concentrate all of your attention on listening. Don't interpret or evaluate what you hear. It just *is*. If your mind wanders away, bring it back to raw listening. Try perceiving the soundscape in layers. First your own sounds, your breaths and your body's inner workings. Then any individual sounds that come from outside your body, nearby. Then take your attention to places further away, where the sounds are still distinct. Notice them. Awaken your ears to all the indistinct sounds that mesh to make the wider aural world beyond: perhaps the noise of weather, distant reverberations, the hum and drone of the city. Having built up these audio layers, listen and pay attention to all these sounds at once, but refrain from making stories, explanations or judgements. Keep listening until the timer goes off. Then, if words come to you, write down what you have heard.

If you do this focused activity often enough, you may become generally more sensitive to sound. It's likely that you'll detect more, discern more. Your writing will resonate more. And, I hope, your appreciation of life will be greater.

40
DO TOUCH

Try describing something, anything, without once referring to your sight of it. That means:

- no visual verbs (*it looks like, it appears, it shines, it looms, it casts a shadow, it blocks the view*)

- no colour references

- no references to light or dark

- no two-dimensional aesthetics (say, details in a drawing or in a map)

- no judgement of looks (such as *handsome, ugly, pleasing to the eye*)

What are you left with?

All the other senses.

To avoid becoming lazily dependent on sight, the most convenient of senses, I've promoted the storytelling seductions of sound. I've made much of Nose Power. But what of touch? This is another neglected sense. Yet, in real life, we neglect it at our mortal peril.

Try describing an object, or a place, through touch. Fingertips are the vanguard of touch. Through your hands you feel texture, shape, moisture, friction, temperature. Hands are easy. But your feet feel, and your face feels, and your body feels. Don't forget: even your teeth feel. It's all vital information for this porous, pleasurable, hurtable animal that is the human body.

In the mid-1990s, I was invited to work in Beirut. The city was a landscape of brokenness, poised for reconstruction after years of war. My residing sense-memory is of dust. It was dust and grit everywhere – all over my clothes, in my hair, in my eyes, between my teeth. Out of habit, our guide kept brushing her business suit. Again and again. It was a matter of redistribution. She too was covered in dust. For everyone in the city, on the street, in offices, the texture of those days was gritty. Dust was in every touch.

Remember the jagged hurt of flint under your feet on a pebble beach. Remember the thrum of drums in your gut. Remember the tenderness of a lover's hand trailing soft fingertips along your arm. Remember the shock of a slap, the slipperiness of a river rock, the fuzzy comfort of a childhood blanket, the sting of sunburn. Touch your reader with your touch.

41
SWEET, BITTER, SOUR, SALTY, UMAMI

The wild success of cookery programmes and cookery books says something about taste. Of course it does. It's a kind of storytelling. The story's subject happens to be food. But taste isn't just about food.

Think of the taste in your mouth when you haven't eaten for a long while. Or when you've experienced deep animal fear. Think of the salty taste of your skin after swimming in the sea. The metallic taste of blood. The bitter taste of a hangover. Lick a cough-syrup spoon for a sweetness so sweet it makes you shiver. Writing about sex can be an emotion-free zone if you get too caught up in the physics – what does a lover's body taste like?

Try editing a poem with a certain taste in mind.

Try conceiving a character in terms of a particular taste.

Taste and emotion are close allies. Why does revenge taste sweet? Why do we take things to the bitter end? How does a relationship go sour?

And what of that mysterious taste called umami? Apparently, our first encounter with umami is breast milk. Like a savoury broth, it's the taste of comforting nourishment. I wonder what emotions we taste in the womb.

Explore taste, observe it, and enjoy every moment of your tastebuds in action. Spend a day doing the things you'd normally do, all the while noticing your own sense of taste, as well as any references to taste around you – conversations, advertising, signage, art. Fill your notebook with the day's tasting notes, each and every one. This is likely to be a potent verbal concoction once it's done.

Now that you've activated your taste detector, leave it on. You can make yourself hungry for more of life, and you can make your reader hungry for more of your writing.

42
THE SOUNDS OF SILENCE

As a writer, it's your job to listen as consciously as a monk.

Turn off your vision for a moment, subdue your power of smell, and listen.

What do you hear? Silence? Never. In our physical world, silence doesn't exist.

On the set of a film shoot, I learned that the production sound mixer reliably makes a recording of the ambient sound before and after the action is filmed. The cast and crew remain quiet for a time. This is to capture each scene's unique background sound, an audio substrate that will be needed later on, especially if additional dialogue recording needs to be layered in.

During post-production, working with the re-recording mixer and sound editors on the final edit, I learned that even a tiny gap in the soundtrack, a 'hole' that is technically a silence, feels like a dull thud of pressure in the ears. It almost hurts. It has to be filled with low-level indeterminate noise, or some of that ambient audio from the shoot.

Listen to the compositions of Antonio Vivaldi or Arvo Pärt, and think of silence as an instrument in the orchestra; it provides space for other instruments to be heard. Composers as different as Claude Debussy and Miles Davis have suggested that music is what happens *between* the notes. John Cage famously created a composition called *4'33"*. Musicians performing this work do not play instruments or make deliberate sounds; they do nothing but be present for 4 minutes and 33 seconds. The audience completes the work by listening attentively. What do you hear? The orchestra of your body. The world around you. That is the music.

Silence is not golden, it's every colour. It's beautiful, full of possibilities. Think of the positive space between words in T.S. Eliot's *Four Quartets*, or the structural silence in Samuel Beckett's plays. As you write, imagine using silence in this conscious way. You might hear the universe, just being. Perhaps that is the sonic performance, the ambient music, to accompany your words. Or you might have a deliberate soundscape in mind. What is the background sound of your words?

What happens in the rests and pauses?

What is positively left unsaid?

How can we use silence to provide space for the words and feelings of others?

43
YOU NEED ONLY ONE VIOLIN

Vivaldi wrote that if you find the word *solo* written in a concerto, it must be played by one violin only. In *Notes on the Cinematographer*, film-maker Robert Bresson repeats the message: 'not to use two violins when one is enough'.

These are wise words.

But now I'm being a turncoat. One minute I'm all for verbal profligacy. Spend, spend, spend, I say, don't be precious. Next minute, I'm chucking out violins and leaving gaps in the orchestra.

That's because now I'm thinking about editing, not writing.

First we conquer the blank page and get ideas foaming, expanding, filling up the spaces. Then we go back and cut. Both processes are essential.

There's usually a fair bit of cutting to do.

Less is more.

And purging – as decluttering experts will tell you – feels marvellous.

44
THE TRUTH ABOUT CLICHÉS

Clichés are works of genius because they are great and true and everlasting. The first few times a cliché-to-be is uttered, the listener must be amazed at the precision of it, the fresh resonance. It fizzes with power. The first *babbling brook* made pictures and sounds: Nature possessed of a mind and a will, water talking. Now we don't really see it or hear it. Like other budding clichés, it's so good that it is quoted, repeated and repeated, again and again. Until we stop paying attention.

Every important emotion is prone to cliché. That's why it's so hard to write sincerely about love, lust, sex, birth, death, anger, fear, crying, fighting, remembering. *Memories came flooding back. It seemed like only yesterday. The town was picture-postcard perfect. She loved him more than words could say, with every fibre of her being. The happy couple tied the knot. They fought like cat and dog. His eyes glazed over. She clung to him for dear life, but he gave up the ghost. It was the last twist of the knife…* Actually clichés are quite fun when they're crowded together like this. It's almost a costume party.

My mistress' eyes are nothing like the sun – Shakespeare relishes romantic clichés, especially when he subverts them.

> *I have seen roses damask'd, red and white,*
> *But no such roses see I in her cheeks;*
> *And in some perfumes is there more delight*
> *Than in the breath that from my mistress reeks.*

For other writers, unironic clichés can slip in slyly, hoping that no one will notice. They infiltrate. And, like ideology, they are invisible to their owners. George Orwell talks about dying metaphors, those worn-out images and phrases that are no longer evocative. His judgement: ugliness, staleness, laziness of thought, imprecision. Oh yes, and misuse. All too frequently, those poor dying metaphors are twisted out of their original meaning.

It's not just phrases or metaphors that succumb to cliché. Characters can be literary stereotypes. Plots can get chained up too. How often have you heard a disappointed person say: 'And you just *knew* what was going to happen next'? This is not because the story itself needed to be changed. Romeo and Juliet can still fall in love, be star-crossed and die. There's life in them yet. A clichéd story is one that needs to be told differently.

Complacency gets in the way of creativity. Use your heart and belly and brain to write. Make the telling fresh and yours. You'll pay attention. And others will pay attention. Win-win.

45

DESCRIBING WITHOUT DESCRIPTION

Elmore Leonard, the brain behind the novels *Get Shorty, Jackie Browne, Killshot* and others, likes to cut qualifiers out of his prose. It's easy to see why his novels translate so well into screenplays. If you cut adverbs and adjectives, you're left with dialogue and action.

Such an approach doesn't mean that your prose becomes undescriptive. In fact, action can be a subtle and effective way of describing – which is why I invite student-writers to try it.

> *In this room, my grandmother sang me to sleep.*
>
> *Here I listened to a strange grunting from my parents' room at night. It sounded like they were fighting. Later, they really did fight and, as I lay in bed, the streetlamp light just visible through the gaps in the curtains, I could hear. Voices, quiet and gruff at first, then louder, then a thud, a crash, a squeal, then silence. For hours.*

Then days. Then for years, after Dad left.

Above my bed, on the bookshelves my dad had put up, were the classics and pulp novels I acquired and read over and over in the teenage years. In the cupboard near the door were the toys I was now too old for and, hidden underneath, the magazines I was too young for.

When I got the scholarship, I took the letter to this room and read it. I read it twenty times at least, then went next door and told my mother. She had a hangover, so wasn't really listening.

No one in the class has any trouble picturing this room, even though the writer uses events rather than adjectives to shape the place. We don't just visualize; we feel the room.

Many of us go further. We see the layout of the house. I'm sure we all have slightly different places in mind, rendered with personal details of places we know and remember. But as long as the writer's room stays constant (because he has thoroughly imagined the space inside and out before using it as the setting for action), I continue happily to inhabit this hybrid location, this halfway house between his room and my version of it – until he 'moves' a chair or 'builds' a wall, and I adjust to his vision.

How does action 'describe' a room? If a character paces at length, we don't need to be told that the space is not tiny or cramped. If the character's footsteps echo, we instantly imagine hard surfaces, a lack of clutter. Each verb, each action and reaction, describes without using overt description.

Try writing, or rewriting, a description without using adjectives. What happens? The picture will take on a different emotional tone.

Try your hand at writing, or rewriting, a scene without using adverbs. *He walked slowly* might become *he walked*. Or *he ambled. He limped. He dragged his feet.* Each version is different in meaning and effect.

Few writers are quite so spartan as Elmore Leonard and it's a tough order to make a whole novel out of action and dialogue. It's likely to be shorter than the average volume, which is no great loss. But what does this approach gain? It's a dynamic way of expressing one part of the narrative (like 2+2), while letting us decide – with joyful satisfaction – what it adds up to.

46
ACTION THROUGH DESCRIPTION

Action is often pitted against description. The assumption is that action is important and exciting, while description is pleasant and ornamental. The other assumption is that action and description are diametrically opposed. Like fast and slow. Like dynamic and static. But, just as you can describe without using overt description, you can use description to convey action.

T.S. Eliot wrote of the 'objective correlative' in an essay about *Hamlet*, noting how, in art, external events and situations and objects should evoke, even formulate, a particular emotion. Inspired by Eliot, and by writer-teacher John Gardner, I ask students to describe a scene through a character's point of view, conveying the character's emotional state without explicitly identifying it, and without telling us what has occurred to cause the emotional state. This is more than the pathetic fallacy, where a character's psychological state is projected onto the world – say, the weather seems violent and grim because the character is feeling violent and grim. This is more than a state of mind writ large. It's an oblique approach to storytelling, and it's an immersive pleasure for writer and reader alike.

In poetry or prose, show us a character who is waiting in a public place, having just learned momentous (good/bad) news about a loved one. Don't reveal the actual news to us. Writing from the third-person point of view, describe the external facts of the scene – the place, physical sensations, other people, noticed details – as your character perceives them. Let us figure out for ourselves what has happened.

Once you've practised this subtle storytelling skill, try listening actively to what people feel but don't explicitly say.

47

HOW NOT TO FEAR PLOT

Many writers are daunted by plot, the art of choosing and arranging the events that best tell a story. How to sequence the telling so that one event leads causally to another, how to choose what to foreshadow or protract, and when to reveal what information?

Certain fears make sense for our survival (it's a good idea not to rattle a rattlesnake) but, let's face it, plots don't hurt. When you conquer your fear of plot, you'll be conquering plot. As with many other dispensable fears, it can be tamed by understanding, confronting and doing – whereupon you're likely to feel wiser, stronger and more capable. Happy days!

What is a good story? And what is plot? There are numerous experts who have devoted themselves to answering these questions. I won't attempt to miniaturize that vast body of work in this chapterette. But I will offer practical ways of overcoming some of the most common plot-based insecurities. As ever, they're for you to pick and mix – or disregard.

Get some narrative drive

Think kinetics. Forward motion, and an oppositional force: friction. This is the crucial conflict. Even when you have an identifiable protagonist, an agent of action, it's easy to be waylaid by detail and the unexpected tributaries of story that emerge as your writing flows. I have a 'potted biography' exercise that has helped me and innumerable student-writers over the years. It goes like this. Think of the character. Make brief bullet points of key details, such as age, setting, context. Note a few salient physical characteristics. Note a few salient psychological characteristics. Note something/s your character has to do – it may be a matter of aspiration or compulsion. It may be a dream, a desire or a need, perhaps a matter of vocation, or a quest, perhaps a requirement or a duty. Now you have the forward momentum for plot. Note something/s holding your character back from achieving this: obstacles, real or imagined. People. Limits. Laws. Beliefs. Emotions. Self. Reality. Now you have the friction, the conflict. And reader engagement.

Plan it a bit or a lot

Anything at all can happen in a story – regardless of what is possible or probable in real life – as long as it makes sense within the world of the narrative. You may find it helpful to start plotting with an inciting incident, an event or situation that hooks the reader and triggers other events. If you have a scene or an idea, it needs to be unpacked with questions such as *Why? Why does this matter? What's at stake? And so? And so? And so?* – until the sequence of situations leads towards an ending. The key idea may in fact be the ending, in which case you can work backwards or plot a path towards it. I think of all this as a bit of temporary scaffolding to be dismantled or adjusted as you build your narrative. Don't underestimate how much retrofitting you may need to do. One writer-friend puts it this way: 'Very often I get to the end of a story and realize I need to go back and seed plot elements that will bloom later on.' Some people plan much more intensively, with spreadsheets and timelines – whatever floats your boat/plot.

Cheat

Instead of trying to dream up a story, you can make use of an existing one – your own life, directly or indirectly. Alternatively, you can take inspiration from other people's storylines. This is not theft so much as repurposing, and there are elegant ways to do it. You can use biographies and news stories as armature for your creation – then it's up to you to explore character, to order the telling of events, to decide what and when to foreshadow, delay, extend or reveal. Shakespeare borrowed histories, chronicled lives and legends for many of his plays. Novelist Jane Smiley in turn borrowed from Shakespeare, critically reimagining his *King Lear* in *A Thousand Acres*. You can create new stories from existing fictions, building major characters from minor ones, just as the protagonist of Jean Rhys's *Wide Sargasso Sea* began as a cameo in *Jane Eyre*. Imagining the world through Antoinette's point of view, Rhys released an unheard female voice – the other woman, a mistreated outsider, a 'mad creature in the attic' – unpicking her like a hidden jewel from the weave. And so, from a patriarchal, colonial story, a brilliant new story was created.

Crowdsource

Many brains make plot work. Scriptwriting is often a team effort. All those TV series you know and love are the result of people meeting and working together, bouncing ideas off each other, organizing story elements into different shapes, not being precious. Novelists and other writers can also join forces in this way. You'll need a writing group, workshop or class. Tell them your storyline if you have one, tell them about your ideas and characters, share your concerns, and brainstorm plot like there's no tomorrow. Beyond generating ideas, focused discussion will help you to spot and repair plot holes.

Flout plot

Resist the conventions. Forget the formulas. Write free-form essays and meditations. Write fragments. Be experimental. Play with form. Write poetry where you can contemplate – at length – the evocative properties of a vase or a songbird (no plot). There are wondrous works of fiction that are carried, not by plot, but by the voice and unique perspective; a favourite of mine is Julie Otsuka's *The Buddha in the Attic.* Try writing a plotless novel, your own *Tristram Shandy* or a new *nouveau roman.* Attempt the episodic adventures of the picaresque, where the implicit links between narrative events are *and then* (rather than *and so).* Write a plotless screenplay. For inspiration, I recommend films as diverse as *Last Year in Marienbad, Eraserhead* and *Le Quattro Volte.*

The 'classic' trail

Some people say that there are only x (a few) stories and y (countless) ways of telling them. Aristotle's ideas of narrative structure continue to circulate in various forms today, typically explaining story in three parts. Think introduction–complication–resolution, which is how essay-writing is regularly taught. Or thesis–antithesis–synthesis. Some say a story has a beginning, middle and end. (This book!) A strong narrative arc usually means that central characters undergo significant change by the end. Stories don't always start at the beginning, and narrative order may be very different from chronological order. Storytelling guides are worth investigating, even if you read the rules in order to break them. *(See the recommended reading on pages 230–233.)*

My own approach to plot

None of the above, and all of the above. Mostly I move tentatively forward, like groping in the dark, not knowing what will come next. The plot tends to emerge, piece by piece, in dreams and daydreams, as I'm unearthing character, and when I'm working into scenes. Once there's a certain critical mass, I know I have to get serious about structuring the narrative. Occasionally I need a bit of group input. All in all, this is a highly inefficient approach, and I don't recommend it to anybody, but it keeps me curious, alert and a little bit scared. So I guess I feel the fear, and do plot anyway.

Two stories

Write a poem, play or prose work based on the idea that all great literature is one of two stories: a person goes on a journey or a stranger comes to town.

48

A POINT OF VIEW

In most novels before the twentieth century, it was usual for the author to travel at will into any character's mind and, at a given moment, tell the reader what to think. Even Charles Dickens, a master of showing, regularly stopped the action for a lengthy portrait, telling readers what his characters were like, inside and out. The pre-modernist author could confidently be an invisible god-like being, hovering somewhere above the story, unidentified as a specific character, but ready to offer explanations, backstory, a useful moral, and a philosophical or historical overview well beyond the grasp of their characters.

Certain events contributed to the shattering of old certainties. World wars, psychoanalytic theory, scientific discovery, the proof of relativity, the feminist revolution, the 'death' of God… What kind of authority could be trusted now? Could truth be universal and objective? Could perception be anything but partial, subjective, relative?

It's no wonder that modernism and post-modernism pursued abstraction, breaking forms and breaking rules, recognizing that any vision must be incomplete and flawed. What a beautiful creative mess we have inherited!

We identify and appreciate different points of view. We've acquired a taste for unreliable narrators, clashing perspectives and multiple plot lines. We like to 'listen in' on dialogue, rather than have it described to us. We don't like being told what the moral of the story is. We enjoy fragmentation and inconclusiveness (although too much can be painful). We question the *authority* of the *author*, even though these two words meaningfully intersect.

So who gets away with omniscience? Writers who are deft, accomplished, utterly knowing. Writers before the twentieth century. God.

It can feel tough to constrain a story's point of view to one, and then perhaps another, character. But think of it as the kind of restraint needed for any well-executed creative act.

First, you acknowledge and understand the partial and relative nature of perception. Second, you know that what is left out is as important as what is put in. Think of a well-edited film. A perfect dish.

Personally, I believe it's tougher to keep omniscience going. It needs to be evenly, restlessly distributed across all the characters. Otherwise, switches of perspective can feel odd and disrupt the reader's sense of immersion – in a non-Brechtian, not-clever way.

Imagine how much less immersive *The Talented Mr Ripley* would be if Patricia Highsmith strayed randomly from Ripley's worldview. Without an omniscient narrator, the intensity of gaze is emotive, dramatic and absorbing.

Carefully paced juxtapositions, one point of view following another, can be the actual motor of story. Think of the sequence of individual voices in William Faulkner's *As I Lay Dying*, Toni Morrison's *Paradise* and Michael Cunningham's *The Hours*. Multiple perspectives create narrative tension, insight, complexity, interest.

Finally, it's worth remembering that no narrator, not even the omniscient sort, gets to have the last word. When you send a story out into the world, you let it go. And you let go. It's a liberating action, with potential for unpredictable reaction. It is now several stories – as numerous as its readers – each with their own point of view. Surprisingly, this total lack of control can feel empowering.

Point of view: you

The singular first-person *I* often suggests the intimate, confessional, partial. Action is limited to what the character knows or witnesses. Think of a virtual camera inside the character's head.

The singular 'third-person restricted' allows for a little more distance, a sense of objectivity – although the story is still being told subjectively through this character's limited point of view. Think of the virtual camera hovering outside the character's head, very very close.

The singular second-person *you* is not widely used. In Latin, the vocative case indicates a calling out (*vox* means *voice*); a person or thing is qualified by being addressed directly. When the word *you* appears on the page, the writer is throwing a direct line out to the reader. What kind of relationship does the 'vocative' establish between storyteller and audience? What written or spoken forms of communication come to mind?

Try writing a poem or short story using the second person singular:

- drawing the listener directly into the narrative, or

- recounting an important event from your childhood, or

- exploring an unfinished relationship.

49
THIRTEEN WAYS OF LOOKING AT A ROOM

Describe a room. It can be any room. Imagined, remembered, dreaded, loved, public, private, empty, full of people, fictional, personal...

Know this room before you start writing about it.

Your audience should be able to know the room as well as you do. They should be able to see it, smell it and feel it.

If you don't know your room inside out, your uncertainty will leak through tiny cracks in the prose.

Describe the same room in 13 different ways:

1. lyrical, descriptive, emotional, poetic

2. empirical, with only objective, measurable or provable information

3. with no allusions, similes, metaphors

4. using no adjectives

5. in a journalistic, hard-news style

6. without any emotion

7. using all senses except sight, but not sightless or lightless

8. through dialogue only

9. through action only

10. from the point of view of a child

11. from the point of view of an alien

12. from the point of view of an insect

13. before and after an untold event.

Each of these restrictions creates specific effects, and reveals important information about the perceiver.

50
'‎I AM A WRITER'

It took me years and years to admit to being a writer. I used to worry that if I said it, plain and simple, just like that, I might sound vain or deluded. But it had become almost silly to hide my writing side. Slowly but surely, the evidence had piled up. Even now, I say that I am 'mostly a writer'. Many of my writer-friends are similarly cautious. Why?

Is it because we have to earn a living, and creative writing must fit into the spaces after the 'proper' work is done? Is it because writing can look like a hobby until we're officially published? Many actors spend as much time between roles as they do performing on stage or screen, although they still define themselves as actors. And people who have a leisure pursuit – say, photography – will merrily utter the words 'I'm a photographer', even if they don't take photographs all day, every day.

Creative writing may be a hobby, a course of study, an aspiration, a vocation, a career – perhaps a little of all these things, without being definitively one or the other. Is it because of this in-betweenness that we fumble with self-definition?

I think there's something else going on. It's fear. Fear of ridicule, fear of criticism, fear of rejection.

The emotional logic goes like this: I'll focus on my day-job because there I have the fact of employment, waged or unwaged. Writing doesn't matter so much. I'll minimize my creative writing, and then it won't be too bad if I make a mess of it.

Many of the chapters in this book are about dismantling the different fears that attach themselves to writers. If you unpack your fear, if you think it through, if you learn to stare it down, you'll be able to minimize this negative emotion rather than minimizing your writing side. If you acknowledge the fear and write like a wild thing anyway, you'll be writing yourself happy. Don't worry if you don't yet think of yourself as a writer.

The philosopher Epictetus would tell you, plainly and simply: if you wish to be a writer, write.

51
SIMPLE IS CLEVER

I remember a maths teacher at school writing out a long and beautiful proof that filled the blackboard. His commentary as he wrote was as natural in its forward momentum as *The House that Jack Built*. There were white chalky brackets within brackets, fractions piling up in layers, and squares throwing their roots out all over the place. At least, that's how I remember it. The teacher carried on in perpetual scribbling motion until the finale, a satisfying series of crossings out. This phrase equalled that, and this operation cancelled that one out, cross, cross, slash, slash. What was left? A short, sweet, simple thing: $e=mc^2$. Ah, the beauty of it. The tiny enormity of it.

In philosophy, there are searches for universal definitions. Say, of beauty. Or pleasure. There is never an answer as simple as an all-purpose algebraic formula. But ideas can be reduced to simple truths, even if the simplicity of those truths hide verbal pile-ups of history, detail, experience, example, exception, the complications of context.

Writing and thinking are acts of complication. But don't forget how beautiful complication can be when it is concentrated into simplicity. The equation $e=mc^2$ is sublime in its simplicity.

Simple is not simplistic.

Simplicity is often complication in disguise.

You can read and re-read William Blake's 'The Tyger', Adrienne Rich's 'A Mark of Resistance', or 'The Red Wheelbarrow' by William Carlos Williams, despite the simplicity of these poems – no, *because* of their simplicity. In the world of copywriting for design or advertising, writers are not usually paid per word. In fact, fewer words can be more potent. Short phrases can last long in the public memory. *Just do it. Think different.* It seems indelicate to talk about poems and slogans in the same breath but, in both cases, multifaceted thought is concentrated into a few well-chosen words.

Start writing about an idea. Write freely, expansively, thoughtfully. Don't worry about form or genre. Take the writing to its natural conclusion, however long. Pause – sleep on it. Now condense it. Reduce it. Concentrate it. Condense it again. Keep going until you have reduced it to its essential elements.

Might this become a fleeting but formidable poem, or a searing work of flash fiction? Perhaps you'll arrive at a title or a 'mantra' that will resonate throughout a longer work, in the way that *Catch-22* does, or *The Unbearable Lightness of Being*.

It may be enough to keep your writing as a fragment, intense and highly coloured, like a single piece from an incomplete mosaic.

52
SHOW NOT TELL?

I like to refer to cinema when I teach creative writing. Films are how I write and how I dream. Film-makers know that a story is born again when it is edited. And, some time after modernists wrote off the omniscient narrator, fiction-makers co-opted the cinematic mantra: *show not tell*.

Some people might balk at this. They'd say that films are all surface, that short stories and novels can travel inside the mind (Proust can devote pages to cake-induced reverie), and film adaptations of books always leave the brainy grey matter out.

Another objection to the *show-not-tell* mantra is this: conspicuous telling has its uses, especially if you're concerned to draw attention to form and the constructed nature of any story. There are subtleties of thought and feeling that cannot really be externalized, and there are countless pleasures to be had in the choice and arrangement of words.

Showing is incomplete. Of course it is, ask any conjurer. It's against the rules of any decent magicians' union to *tell*. Don't you die a little when you hear about the fake card or false bottom? It's just as disappointing when captions or voice-overs try to tell you the meaning of life, the universe and everything.

And yet many of us can't resist the urge to explain. Is this a hangover from school-essay days, or a habit of writing we've learned at the office?

Sometimes it springs from our fear that the audience won't understand what's going on. We slide into summary mode. And we tidy it all up with a conclusion. The end. Oh dear. The end of immersive pleasure. Inessential exposition is a dependable way of breaking a spell.

When you notice that you're explaining a story or a character, try showing instead. Here's a tiny example: if a character is feeling nervous, maybe they'll fidget or sweat a lot. Maybe they'll snap at someone, or crash the car.

This showing approach is useful even where you don't have the luxury of pictures, say, when you're writing a podcast or radio drama. That nervous character can be audibly fidgety, they can snap at someone (dialogue) and they can crash the car (sound effects). The character can 'show' nervousness through difficulty of speech, a dry mouth, a strained voice, jumbled words, stammering, hesitating. Even perspiration can be 'shown' when another character remarks on it. Gestures, actions, symptoms, incidents – they are usually more enticing than a writer standing in front of the text saying 'this character feels nervous'.

We enjoy the illusion of judging motivation and meaning for ourselves. It is an illusion because the author is the conjuring authority behind the text, but now that conjurer is compelled to *be* a character, or to hide behind characters, and resist the urge to explain the how and why.

Your greatest fiction might be that your story unfolds and develops in the reader's or listener's mind, without apparent authorial intervention.

Imagine scenes. Put characters into scenes. Let them reveal something of themselves in scenes, without stopping to deliver lengthy sermons on behalf of the writer. Think of the story that advances within each scene, and then the story between scenes.

Pay attention to the telling, but lean towards showing.

53
MOVING IMAGES

It makes sense for the writer and the reader to see images. More than a third of the human brain is devoted to processing visual information. We are hardwired to favour visual perception.

Even so, new writers tend to get stuck on philosophical ruminations and bureaucratic terminology – big abstract words – because polysyllabic Latinate vocabulary (as shown here) has a way of sounding important.

But remember the hot air balloon that launches Ian McEwan's novel *Enduring Love*. It launches the film adaptation too, and rightly so. It's an utterly compelling image. It stays in the mind and energizes the novel from beginning to end. Remember the albatross of the Ancient Mariner. Remember the Holy Grail, the yellow brick road, the secret garden, the scarlet letter, the color purple, the tell-tale heart. Remember the picture of Dorian Gray.

As totems, as icons, even as souvenirs, images can concentrate meaning and generate story.

Try seeing yourself as a visual artist making pictures with words.

Better still, make moving pictures with your words.

Take some cues from cinema: establishing shots, framing, tracking, lighting, zooming, focusing, dissolving, freezing, cutting. Slow motion, speed. Scenes, sequences of scenes. Movement within scenes, movement between scenes.

If you're starting a short story, you could think of your first lines as an establishing shot. What does the reader need to know about this world before they venture further, and who is this story about?

In the medieval poem *Sir Gawain and the Green Knight*, the interior seduction scenes are dramatically juxtaposed – intercut, piece by piece – with the exterior hunting scenes, inviting us to draw parallels between two kinds of prey in a premeditated pursuit. In Emily Dickinson's poetry, the dashes frequently act as freeze-frames and jump cuts. In Jim Crace's novel *Being Dead*, tiny creatures at work decomposing two undiscovered corpses are watched in extreme close-up, as if using a slowly moving macro lens. In David Foster Wallace's essay 'Consider the Lobster', the gaze is like a steady camera moving onwards at an even speed, revealing details of biology, consumption, marketing and excess, in sharp focus and bright light; the lengthy footnotes feel like elaborate cutaways.

The practice of creative writing is likely to intensify your gaze, as you write and as you live. Pay attention to your visual world and the kinetic energy of things, the movement within and between events, the traffic of perceptions.

54
MIND THE GAP

Those of us who live or work in London are familiar with the resonant voice of the Underground god that commands us to MIND THE GAP when the train doors open. It's an existential line. It is repeated, like an incantation.

Familiar though it is, the disembodied command does make me look for the gap when the tube train pulls in. Sure enough, there it is, the straight train's edge next to the curve of the platform. Or the unmatched levels of station and train floor. Like everyone else, I step with care over the gap, having minded it.

Film editors think of editing as piecing fragments together, often fragments that don't fit. This is a useful way of rethinking the notion that a story flows seamlessly from beginning to middle to end. It doesn't. The gaps between unmatched levels and ill-fitting edges are doing much of the storytelling work.

When I watch any film I try to look at the editing. I look at the jumps, the transitions, the non sequiturs. Why does one scene dissolve slowly into the next? Why does another scene fade to black? How and when does the camera's perspective get switched? Why does an image disappear with a swift cut to another image – what has happened invisibly in between?

Accomplished film editors have an instinctive feel for disruption. It's not just about being stylish. Gaps are good – as long as they're a positive creative choice, not a case of authorial fudging or avoidance.

Creative writers can learn some good crafty lessons from the way films are pieced together. The temptation when you're writing is to join everything up and smooth over the edges. This is because you're being kind to your readers – too kind. They'd prefer to mind the gap.

Think of the way good film editors work. Let your readers enjoy reading between the lines.

Here's a writing exercise to mind the gap.

Write a portrait of a character. Describe, describe, describe. Put this description aside.

Start again: portray this same character using only action and/or dialogue.

Start again: show this same character from another character's point of view.

What insights, what stories, are yielded by the parts that don't fit, the gap between the two perspectives?

55
AN ARGUMENT AGAINST TRUTH

'But it's true!'

I don't think I've sat through one creative writing class without hearing those words.

So it's true.

So what?

Just because it's true, that doesn't mean it's credible.

'But it actually happened – to me!'

Just look at the frowns on their foreheads. If your audience is saying 'I don't believe it' or 'I don't trust it', then the writing has to work harder to make it more convincing for them. You won't always be there to chaperone your text, to present the case for its authenticity.

If a coincidence feels implausible, despite its truth, you might need to set it up so that it doesn't seem so outlandish. Coincidence can be a satisfying spur to get a story going; towards the end of a tale, coincidences can feel like authorial cheating. If a factual event seems unbelievable, reflect on what needs to be said that normalizes the event within its context, making it possible, even inevitable.

Still, is it enough for a story to be true?

Just because it's true, that doesn't mean it's engaging.

Work out how best to convey the truth of your tale, drawing on your creative skills and pushing beyond the obvious. Try not to let the literalness of the content weigh down the expressiveness of the form. Let your inventiveness off the leash.

56
LAWLESS TERRITORY

There is a lawless land between the defined territories of Fiction and Fact. In the lawless land, a wife finds out about her real-life husband's affair when she reads his published novel. A renowned artist is maligned after death by a bitter family member whose memoir is made into a film. Following divorce, a couple's problematic sex life is laid bare in intimate detail; the author calls it creative non-fiction. Long before defamation, slander and libel, there's plain hurt.

A writer-friend of mine talks of using people as models, in the way that visual artists do. He's not referring to portrait-making, where an artist's primary aim is to create an image of a sitter. He's thinking of the artist's mate who appears in a fresco, holding up a grand ceiling with mythological muscles, or the servant girl whose face is a study for the Madonna.

The model analogy is interesting. When a painter's sitter sits, they can expect to see an artwork depicting something of their likeness. They may not like the actual image, but presumably they have chosen or agreed to participate in the artistic process.

However, characters don't *sit* for us, except in interviews. And writers, as we know, are thirsty sponges. We absorb bits of people all the time without them noticing; we ourselves may not notice we're doing it.

Just how we balance our art and our relationships is a matter of personal choice, but no amount of creative licence justifies being a literary louse. We can make it our intention to be imaginative and compassionate, especially when our creative work is inspired in some way by people we know. Chances are, we'll sleep well too.

57
THE ART
OF POETRY

Think of a figurative image and an abstract one. I'm going to picture the familiar portrait of King Henry VIII by Hans Holbein the Younger, and *Blue Poles (Number 11, 1952)* by Jackson Pollock. In each case, we are invited to perceive the aesthetic qualities of the artwork: light, texture, colour, composition, emotional effect… In the first painting, we are looking for a likeness of the real person, a record of his presence, which is as informative as a photograph. In the second painting, the artist is not interested in reproducing or representing a likeness. He's more interested in painterly gesture, the qualities of his medium and even the texture of the canvas.

If words represent things, as painting represents things, then there are some writing styles that are more figurative or prosaic, and others that are more abstract or poetic. You could say that commercial genre writers tend to use language as a neutral means of portraying character and conveying plot. By contrast, you could say that James Joyce works like an abstract artist in his novel *Finnegans Wake*. His language creates impressionistic textures, while narrative events and character motivation are opaque.

Somewhere in between the literal and lateral, you'll find two of my favourite authors: Michael Ondaatje and Annie Proulx. They care about the aesthetic properties of words, and they care about telling a good story. Analyze the poetic prose of *The English Patient*, or *The Collected Works of Billy the Kid*. Dive into *The Shipping News*, or *Postcards*.

Poetry revels in its own visual and aural textures, alliteration and assonance, rhythm and rhyme, the music within and between sentences. Prose can do likewise.

Roll your references in colour. Create a stir with sounds. Relish the cultural, visual and aural properties of words. Love language.

58
CLASH OF
THE TONGUES

In class we hear a romantic story peppered with phrases straight from the business desk. *A daily occurrence. Our respective abodes. A date that proved mutually successful.* I check with the student-writer about his language. Is this a character with bureaucracy on his mind, despite the excitement of a new romance? If yes, we need to hear this voice consistently throughout the story, and it needs to be heightened until it becomes uncomfortable or funny.

I'm interested in this idea of bureaucratic love. The conventions of romantic literature would have us expect other things. Mellifluous metaphors. Semantic swoons. How delicious it would be to ramp up the romance with a ton of his-and-hers respective filing and mutually convenient howsoevers. Nikolai Gogol and Franz Kafka both knew how to go wild, if not romantic, within the administrated confines of the office.

Clashing tongues can make for memorable stories.

Sarah by J.T. LeRoy (Laura Albert) gains extra energy by pitching the child-protagonist's narration – simple syntax, first-person present tense, jaggedly poetic vernacular – against the adult dialogue of truckers and sex workers, and the unexpectedly lavish descriptions of gourmet dishes at the truck-stop diner: calf liver reduction sauce, fresh corn ragout, work of art pecan soufflé, crème fraîche strudel…

Julie Otsuka's *When the Emperor Was Divine* is a work of historical fiction about the experiences of a Japanese American family sent to an internment camp during World War II. The language throughout is consistently unsentimental, pared down to an exquisite minimum. The story wrapped me in silence. I was enthralled. My emotions were swallowed and suppressed. And then came the last chapter. What a shock. A howl of outrage, a stream of internalized abuse, a chapter that shouts and rants and doesn't seem to pause for breath until the very last word. When I closed the book's cover, I knew I wasn't closing the story or putting it away somewhere forgettable and indifferent. The story had blasted a hole in my world.

Try these two exercises in flexing and clashing language:

1. Describe a disease with loving lyricism.

2. Describe a flower with violent fear and loathing.

In each case, consider mood, subtext, momentum, implicit backstory. Who is the narrator? Whose perspective is conveyed?

59

A METAPHOR IS LIKE...

Once, during a trip to Paris, I was in a hotel lift with two other guests who were studying the buttons, bewildered.

'*Étage!*' one of them said in exasperation. 'How on earth does anyone come up with a word like *étage* for *floor*?'

All language is metaphoric in the sense that words stand for something else, and we often forget this, confusing the word with the thing itself. In his painting *The Treachery of Images*, René Magritte painted a pipe with the caption: *Ceci n'est pas une pipe*. This is not a pipe. His painting could have been called *The Treachery of Words*.

Why do we add to the 'treachery' by talking about one thing while alluding to another? Why would Robert Burns write 'My love's like a red, red rose, that's newly sprung in June' and why would Shakespeare write 'Shall I compare thee to a summer's day'? Throughout *Orlando*, Virginia Woolf plays wryly with the idea that a writer – constantly questing for the ideal metaphor – is a person for whom everything is something else. But it's not just word workers who use metaphor, simile, synecdoche, personification, metonymy...

Scientists and historians use metaphoric imagery to make remote or inaccessible concepts feel comprehensible. *The Amazonian rainforests are the world's lungs. The plum pudding model of the atom was superseded by the mini solar system model.*

Journalists and reviewers use metaphor to speed up and condense. *This café is a Mecca for coffee-lovers.* The allusion here evokes the concept of a holy site, a destination for reverent pilgrims, a place that is sure to be crowded – all with one short intensifying word.

Politicians use metaphor and simile to simplify complex ideas and to persuade us to think in certain ways. Leaders appoint 'tsars' – drug tsars and crime tsars – to convince us that they mean business; the familiar names (say, *policy director*) don't have half as much emotive power. It is for this reason that an over-used figure of speech – *it felt like an eternity* – fails in its aim to intensify meaning or emotion.

In the first pages of Fyodor Dostoevsky's novel *Crime and Punishment*, we read that Raskolnikov sleeps in a coffin-shaped room, and we start to feel, uneasily, the imminence of death. The repetition of the coffin image carries with it a kind of obsessiveness. The analogy conveys character, theme, even plot, by permeation rather than explicit narration. If Dostoevsky had described his protagonist's bedroom as an intriguing polygon, we might have inferred that Raskolnikov is untroubled and mathematically minded, perhaps a student of architecture – and so, perhaps, no crime, no punishment, a different story.

Compare the different effects of these simple examples: *Her dress was red. Her dress was as red as blood. Her dress was whirling, red, an autumn leaf. Her dress was the red of a bride's dress, lucky and joyful. Her dress was red, like a warning. Her dress – was it primary red or vermilion? Her dress was party-political flag-waving red. Her dress was the colour of a red, red rose.* Individually, each example transmits specific meaning by analogy. Piled up together like this, the analogies send us in confusing and conflicting directions – which is why it's generally a good idea not to mix metaphors, and not a good idea to use them unwittingly.

So what's the point of transferring the properties of one thing to another?

To convey character, theme, atmosphere – even plot – by inference rather than reference.

To describe the indescribable – and so to communicate its attributes.

To make the familiar unfamiliar, and so to see it afresh.

To make the unfamiliar familiar, and so to understand it.

To transfer emotion, and so to influence.

To condense and contract, and so to intensify the aesthetic effect.

All these are within your metaphoric power. Use your power sparingly.

This is not a pipe, it's a proposal. Spend a day doing the things you'd normally do, while noticing the metaphors and similes around you: in conversation, messages, signage, advertising, news, games, words, images… Analyze what effects are intended or created.

60
FOUND IN TRANSLATION

'Forgive me. I assassinate your language,' says Guillem, before sharing his vivid writing with the class. Khadiza reads out her evocative tale of the misspelling in her name. In Takayo's prose short story, silent fearful pauses are shown as '. . .' and Yasmeen is reminded of manga.

Samuel Beckett wrote his best plays in French. By choice. Because it was good for him, like exercise. It made his writing muscles work. He must have been rather good at French, but it was first and foremost a foreign language. It was the vaccine against cliché. He wanted to stop the fluent from flowing. He compelled himself to think quite carefully about every word before he committed. Each little parcel of letters was harder to come by, and a bit strange. It felt new.

The translator's journey is a garden of forking paths.

Do you opt for the word that most closely matches the literal meaning of your original? Does that mean you lose some poetry in the process? Alliteration, assonance, the splish and splash of onomatopoeia, rhythm, rhyme... all of these create aural texture. And the shape of words –

the way they look on the page, how long, how short, how round, how spiky, how many – that's visual texture too. Then there's the freight of association: does this word have a whiff of history about it, the smell of old leather and brittle paper? Does this other word (which means almost the same thing) sound like something from the corporate world, spoken by a slick executive? Perhaps this word has been ensnared by TV or politics – a good or bad thing, depending on context. And this other synonym, well, it's been so overused, so exhausted of purpose, nobody seems to notice it any more.

Of course, the trick (even though you're writing in your own language) is to *think foreign*. It's a two-way glass: flip it this way, then that. Be a stranger to each word and size it up. Being foreign to your usual words can release new meanings from them. New textures. New emotions. New stories.

Multilingual writer and literary critic George Steiner compared language to vision: one language gives you sight, but two give perspective. Delve into words like a translator and see what possibilities you find.

61
TAKE YOUR MOUTH FOR A WALK

We discover and learn things when we say them. The process of articulation helps us not just to organize thought, but to generate thought. That's why we like to talk things through with others, surely? In the process of utterance we explore, clarify and reach new insight. Maybe this is what Dadaist Tristan Tzara meant when he wrote that ideas are formed in the mouth.

We need dialogue. Stories need dialogue. We miss dialogue when it's not there. It's like an open window or a blast of fresh air in the 'closed' text that is narrative prose. Think of that feeling you have as you're reading: the story seems to open up when the characters speak. White spaces appear, and somehow the sound becomes louder, clearer. But poor dialogue lets down an otherwise good story. Some writers fear it, avoiding it wherever possible and battling with it when they must.

The best way to tackle the challenge of dialogue head-on is to say it out loud. This sounds obvious, doesn't it? But dialogue must be sayable. And it's only when you say it (not just in your mind's ear) that you really hear music, colour, rhythm and voice.

Pretend you're writing a script to be read out by actors, with no prose narrative in between the utterances. You can't go leaning on the upholstery of description to tell us how or why words are spoken. This means you have to make the dialogue work hard.

Your characters are 'talking', not talking, because dialogue is not real speech, any more than a photo is a real person. What you're creating is an illusion, a condensed representation, without all the fillers of everyday conversation.

After you've finished your scene, edit it. Explain less. Get it shorter. Make the remaining words work harder. Make the gaps between them work harder too. What is not said? How is the mood or meaning changed when certain elements go missing? What happens if you shuffle it up?

Look at the very first scene of *The Social Network*. (It's a wordy script – that's part of Aaron Sorkin's style.) Listen forensically to the vocabulary, timing, syntax, logic, flow. Interesting dialogue rarely plods on in order. People get stuck on the same note. Now and then questions are avoided, not answered. A little word can suddenly topple a storm or unleash a tyrant.

In class, I ask student-writers to choose others to read out their dialogue for them, like the first airing of a play. It's very useful for the author to hear how easy (or not) the process of reading is. Even confident readers might stumble over something because the meaning is unclear or because the words are physically difficult to say. Intuitively they'll modify the dialogue as they go along, just as actors do. They run out of breath if there are no pauses. Pointless repetitions start to feel bothersome. And we all realize that, apart from politicians and other performers, nobody talks for very long without getting interrupted.

If the dialogue is convincing, most readers will pick up on pace, rhythm and even personality within a few moments. Speech patterns emerge, as well as accent, idiosyncrasy, idiom, emotion. The underlying power relations between the voices become more obvious.

When the reading is over, we flesh out the characters behind the spoken words. The dialogue writer is amazed at how much we know, and how much emotion we feel, without the need for a blow-by-blow portrait of age, employment, eye colour and hairdo. We can see context. We can infer subtext. We can tell whether this written scene is a habitual exchange between the characters or a life-changing moment. We sniff out the unresolved stuff too, when the writer admits 'I thought I could get away with that...'

The answer is here: read dialogue out loud, not just in your head. Take your mouth for a walk.

62
EUREKA MOMENTS (LOVE YOUR UNCONSCIOUS)

Legend has it that the Ancient Greek polymath Archimedes leapt naked from his bath and ran into the streets proclaiming *eureka!* because he had suddenly solved an intractable mathematical problem: how to measure with precision the volume of irregular objects. It's no coincidence that he'd been in the bath. Yes, an irregular object (his body) displaced the water level just so. But most importantly, his mind had been relaxing, drifting into that uncontrolled state between consciousness and unconsciousness when inspiration happens.

Many creative people say that they get their best ideas when they're in the bath or shower. Others talk enthusiastically about how inspiration happens in that relaxed state just before falling asleep at night – hence the notebook by the bed. Others wake up with the muse before really waking up – hence the notebook by the bed. Go to sleep with a creative knot, and you'll wake up with an idea untangled.

Some writers think of the story choosing them, not the other way around. William Golding talked of taking dictation from his unconscious, the prose flowing into his writing hand. Jorge Luis Borges asserted that 'writing is nothing more than a guided dream'. Author-journalist Robert Moss notes:

> Australian Aborigines say that the big stories – the stories worth telling and retelling, the ones in which you may find the meaning of your life – are forever stalking the right teller, sniffing and tracking like predators hunting their prey in the bush.

Dreams, inspiration, eureka moments, Sleudian frips… they all come at you from the part of your mind that is not being consciously guarded. Too much rational control and you have something that is academic, rather than artistic. But you don't need to be on the brink of sleep for your defences to be relaxed. Dip into one of these activities to nurture your inspirations.

Meditation

Rather than striving to effect an outcome, just meditate. If you'd rather do something physical, try moving meditation: qigong, tai chi or yoga. Notice, over time, what happens to your wellbeing, not just your writing.

Dream journal

Use that notebook by the bed to record dreams while you remember them, even if it means scribbling in the dark.

Automatic writing

The Surrealists relished this technique for its power to release unadulterated creativity. Hidden treasure. Association. Surprise. Instinct. Like many poets before and after them, they experimented with trance-like states. This is from their manifesto: 'Pure psychic automatism by which one proposes to express, verbally [...] the actual functioning of thought. Dictated by thought, in the absence of all control exerted by reason, and beyond all aesthetic or moral concerns.'

Speed writing

Try writing continuously, for at least 10 non-stop minutes, once a day. The rules are: you don't leave the page, you don't edit, you don't stop to think, you don't cross out, you don't slow down, you don't filter. You just write, continuously. If it helps, start your first sentence with a random prompt or an unfinished thought. *(See Chapter 64)*

Focusing, away from words

Another way of releasing your inner words is to try doing something completely different, ideally non-verbal and focused. Like running. Swimming lengths. Walking for the sake of walking. Listening intently to instrumental music. Practising the art of motorcycle maintenance (or gardening, or tea-making) with moment-by-moment, sensation-by-sensation mindfulness. If you let your poem be, if you let your story unfold, it may write itself. Eureka!

63
THE RICHES OF RANDOMNESS

You know your way to work. You make the same journey every day. You know the fastest route, the likely obstacles, the best exits. Then one day there's a giant random spanner in the works. It makes you do things differently. It's an effort. You have to research and think. You notice specific things for the first time. You discover an interesting place you wouldn't have known about otherwise. You feel like you've woken up. Better still, you feel *provoked*. You have new thoughts, new feelings, new possibilities. Three cheers for the unexpected.

Randomness can be a conspicuous feature of your output. 'Why is a raven like a writing desk?' Alice is asked in Wonderland. Lewis Carroll happily admitted that he didn't have a specific answer to the riddle. His works are marvellous concoctions of association: verbal, conceptual, narrative. Randomness is key to the work of Surrealists, Dadaists, Absurdists and all the writers of 'nonsense literature'.

Randomness can be a useful technique to energize creative processes, even if the results are later ordered and structured.

Writer-director Mike Leigh begins making his films without a script, working with actors as collaborators, using improvisation to allow characters and stories to emerge. Choreographer-dancer Karole Armitage has noted that the accidents of improvisation are often better than the intention of choreography, and worth putting into the final work. Visual artist Francis Bacon thought of painting as an accident from which to choose the best parts. Author William Burroughs had fun with scissors, chopping up his text and shuffling the pieces to create intriguing new sequences of ideas and words. Musician Brian Eno and artist Peter Schmidt devised a series of cryptic prompts called *Oblique Strategies*: you pick a card, any card, to resolve a creative block or dilemma. In the creative industry, brainstorming workshops frequently arrive at the best ideas through a spill of humour, a spontaneous aside, a misunderstood comment, a ricochet of unexpected associations.

You can prompt yourself to write in a new way, about new things, if you set yourself a random exercise or two. Note the first noun that appears at the top of page 38 of the first book you take from your bookshelf. Don't cheat. Stick to that noun from that page in that book. Start writing. Pursue whatever form arises: poem, story, script, song or essay. Stick to that noun as your subject, even if at first it fills you with indifference or discomfort. There's the rub. It's an effort. You have to research and think and notice. You discover. You start to feel excited. You have new thoughts, new feelings, new possibilities. Riches.

64

SOME RANDOM PROMPTS

Explore and release your writing, starting with a random prompt, or an unfinished thought:

The day before my birthday...

The difference between today and tomorrow...

I opened the curtain, and outside...

In the beginning there was...

The false mirror...

On a track in the dark, a car stops and...

I looked into the bag and...

Attempting the impossible...

The meaning of night...

At first I thought...

She said she was leaving, but...

The familiar objects...

Last night I dreamt...

65

ABSOLUTE POWER (LOVE YOUR INTELLECT)

Beethoven's manuscripts, unlike Mozart's, are loaded with blots, corrections and crossings out. There are punctures caused by the jabbing of his pen, angry comments as if speaking to, even bullying, himself. From minor adjustments to entirely rewritten pages, stuck on or sewn in, he worked and reworked his compositions at every creative stage, striving for perfection. But he started with simple ideas, sketches, the inspiration that came to him on walks. In other words, he gave his mind the freedom to roam before crafting with super-conscious intellectual rigour.

Some people are intolerant of writers who say their characters run off and do things. You are the author of your world. You make characters do things. Which of your characters do you despise, which do you neglect, which do you admire? What will you put them through? Is it funny? Does it hurt? What names do you choose for your characters in the first place? These decisions are all within your gift.

As the architect of your universe, you have absolute power. Remember that absolute power corrupts absolutely. Unruly readers like me tend to resist or question an authorial voice dictating, like a despot's loudspeaker in a public square, how to interpret the story. And I am indignant when characters are *as flies to wanton boys* – some author-gods seem unduly cruel in pulling the wings off their creations.

But it's useful to remember Kurt Vonnegut's 'Creative Writing 101' advice. He suggests that you should make awful things happen to your main characters, regardless of how nice they are. This is how your characters will reveal what they're made of, their best and their worst. So whether you're writing fiction or non, screenplay or stageplay, try putting your protagonists to the test. Try bringing their story to a point where they confront the antithesis of themselves, and say things they would not have readily said before, and do things they would never have comfortably done. This happens in ancient myths and modern tales, from *Oedipus* to *The Sopranos*.

Recognize and explore your power. Ask *What if...?* Let your imagination venture to the testing edges, even if you decide to step back when you tell or edit the tale. Such forays into hypothetical discomfort may be enlightening, and not just for your characters.

66

HERDING WORDS

Having acknowledged the absolute power of the creator, we need to remember that, as with all controlling types – parents, bosses, leaders – nobody is divine, and nobody is right all the time. Input from wise advisers is vital.

Editor-poet Ezra Pound cut and shuffled. We can thank him for the Chaucerian spring start to T.S. Eliot's *The Waste Land*. Eliot's wife Vivienne annotated the typescript intensively too. Gordon Lish was why Raymond Carver's fiction became *Carver-esque*. Editing heavily, Lish insisted on paring the prose down to its distinctively minimalist form.

You've allowed your unconscious to roam free, you've created critical mass, an artefact, you've tweaked and tinkered. And then? Long before you get close to a top editor like Pound or Lish, there's a great deal of in-between editing to do.

As your own editor, you need to make your work strange to yourself.

Try any or all of these tactics. Write it longhand. Type it up. Read it out loud. Go through it looking only at structure. Again, just looking at pace. Again, just for plot. Again for style: inelegant or inefficient sentences, unclear phrasing, undesirable excesses, unintended changes of voice, unwanted repetitions. Sift through it, looking at spelling and punctuation, nothing else. Check facts and externally sourced material. Read it out loud again. Print it in a different font, at a different size, in a different layout – it will look strange enough to reveal glitches. Try sleeping on it. (Not literally, unless you're into that kind of thing.) Tomorrow it will be read by a different you. Leave the work for a while, do something else, live life, then come back fresh to the text.

After you, there are other people. Your work is already strange to them, so they don't have to sleep on it or play with fonts. Beyond the critical circle of your writing group, the ideal beta-reader is a well-informed and benevolent bibliophile, someone who's not competitive with you or prone to envy. Brief them thoroughly so that you each know what to expect. Do you need feedback about voice, or form, or theme, or would you rather have nit-picking corrections? The best beta-readers will offer you a multi-layered response. Meet to discuss. Be appreciative, because they have done you a service. Park your ego, listen without interrupting, ask questions, evaluate the feedback and let it settle before editing your work with care. Then appoint your next beta-reader and repeat as necessary.

Finally, there are professionals who charge a fee for their services: literary consultancies, independent editors, book doctors, copy editors and proofreaders. Some people in this field offer mentoring or workshops. Some have links with literary agents and publishers. Check their credentials – appoint an expert, not an enthusiast – and confirm precisely what they will do for the fee.

If you get to the Pound/Lish stage, you'll have an editor at a publishing house who will have a caring overview of your project, as well as an eye for tiny details. They'll work with you to herd the words, steering strays away from danger, guiding all towards happy pastures.

Exercise your in-house editor: write a mini-saga. This literary form is a contradiction in terms because sagas tend to be sizeable in various ways. Enormity of story. Significance of events. Length of time. Extent of detail. Sheer volume of words. Endlessness. In a mini-saga, you're miniaturizing the massive, telling a big tale in just 50 words – with up to 15 additional words for an intriguing, illuminating title. Write the events in whatever order makes a better story, remembering that sequential or chronological order is not always the most effective narrative choice.

Attempt any or all of these options:

- convert a novel (your own / someone else's)
- retell a feature-film story / a full series of feature films
- relate the history of a country / industry / religion / invention / idea
- write your life story, that is, your autobiography.

HAPPY ENDS

In this part of the book, you'll find some *how-to* suggestions (goals, persevering, finishing, the long view), and you'll find plenty of *why-to* ideas: rewards, resilience, resolution and some of the many life-enhancing outcomes that spring from creative writing practice.

67
SUCCESS VS 'SUCCESS'

The Ancient Greek philosopher Epicurus invited us to question each of our desires. He asked himself – and so I ask myself – *what will happen to me if my desire is fulfilled, and what if it is not?*

Publication is a thrill, an exhilarating experience. It's also a distraction, and for some professional writers the publishing journey can lead to a loss of creative freedom. If you want to be published, you'll be happier if your desire to write is greater than your desire to be published.

Do you want to write a bestseller? If so, why? If it's to pay the bills, then I'd suggest you try some other means. There are many surer, faster ways of making a living.

Do you want to gain prestige? I don't recommend chasing success in the outside world, only to feel hollow dissatisfaction on the inside. Publication is a gratifying external acknowledgement of your hard work. Good sales, reviews and awards are icing on the cake. But, like icing, they all melt away, intensely sweet and momentary. Try redirecting your gaze: think from the inside outward.

The point is to write. The joy is in the doing. Discovering yourself, word by word. Unearthing ideas, word by word. Try creating without regard to result. Enjoy the process, how the practice of writing subtly makes its way into how you're living.

Your writing, like your life, is a work in progress.

68

BE A STUDENT FOREVER

The Four Stages of Competence can be a helpful way to think about how people learn skills. You start with unconscious incompetence: you don't know what you don't know. This is the blissful ignorance of the beginner. You move on to conscious incompetence, where you have an idea of the scope and complexity of your mission, your ability falls short of your awareness, and you know how you can improve. Then you develop conscious competence – you know you can do it now, but you really have to concentrate. And finally, you achieve unconscious competence, when you can do something well, almost automatically.

This paradigm, so useful in other aspects of life, doesn't quite square with my idea of creative writing. You are unlikely to be a good writer if you write with unconscious competence.

Creative writing is always a challenge. It always strains and hurts a bit. Unless you're attempting automatic writing or speedwriting, you can never quite turn off. If you do turn off, your writing is likely to be unengaging – in other words, your reader is likely to turn off too.

The engaged and engaging writer stays at an uncomfortable peak of conscious competence. This is not just the position of the amateur. Even seasoned creatives have to concentrate very hard. Thomas Mann believed that writers are people who find writing more difficult than others do. Joseph Heller noted that all the writers he knew had trouble writing. Leo Tolstoy thought you should leave a piece of your own flesh in the inkpot each time you dip your pen.

Don't be troubled by the idea that creative writing is supposed to come 'naturally'. You wouldn't say that about swimming or sculpting. And you wouldn't say any such thing to Pablo Picasso, who had countless ways of insisting that inspiration requires perspiration. Good writing is an effort. This is not a lament. Nor is it a deterrent. It's a kind of consolation. Good writing should always be an effort.

So don't berate yourself if it feels difficult. No matter how confident a writer you are, or how long you've been doing it, you will always, I will always, be struggling like a student.

As creative writers, we can be students forever, purposefully seeking knowledge, striving for growth and understanding, resisting apathy, cultivating awareness, stoking curiosity – our own and others' – always learning. Isn't that a wonderful, vital provocation?

69
LEARN FROM REJECTION

There's a book of mine that lives in the cupboard. It's a manuscript that remains unpublished. It rests on a multi-layered heap of research materials and rejection letters. I refer to this novel as My Broken Book. Student-writers like hearing about it.

My Broken Book was broken all the way through the middle, no matter how much I tinkered with it. I worked and reworked central characters. I radically altered the structure. I rewrote nearly every sentence, obsessing about tone, style, vocabulary. All this happened long after the first draft, which was itself the result of several workings. From the earliest rough jottings through research and final edits, I must have given My Broken Book three years, alongside the day-jobs. Then my literary agent gave it time (reading and sharing) and various publishers gave it time (reading and rejecting).

Rejection made me question why I write. I found answers to that questioning. My Broken Book took me to new places – physically, emotionally, spiritually. I had to write it, and my life is richer now because of it. Through the story I confronted difficult truths, such as death and the business of death. I learned necessary lessons about my craft. It mattered to write to the best of my ability, and that was effortful. It required further effort to accept failure. I understood perseverance. I learned that I want to have writing in my life, regardless of measurable external outcomes.

One day I packed My Broken Book with all its bits and pieces into the cupboard. It was time to move on to the next writing project. I now recognize this work as a transition, a phase of my development. My Broken Book is as vital to me as my published work.

If you have a broken work in the cupboard, please don't wrap it in regret. Don't trouble it with 'If only...' Ask yourself what it has taught you and what you continue to learn from it.

70
GROW YOUNGER

It's not surprising that creative writers find inspiration in the clinical cases described by neurologist Oliver Sacks. Who can forget *The Man Who Mistook His Wife for A Hat*? When the man loses his ability to understand and identify things, the world around him becomes strange and new. His descriptions make us see commonplace objects as if for the first time. He examines a glove as if he has never seen a glove before. He describes its surface, its form, its five *outpouchings*. He wonders if it is some kind of container, perhaps a purse for coins of different sizes.

Familiar objects are transformed, and so we are transformed: we are suddenly, temporarily, unjaded.

When we were children, our perceptions were intense and fresh and new. Standing up. Learning to write. Swimming. Exploring nature. Moments lasted longer then. They glittered hard and bright with detail. We travelled light; our barnacles were few. Our interpretations were feeling, aesthetic. We were not yet anaesthetized by prejudice or familiarity. We experienced wonder.

This is a paradise lost – precisely what creative practitioners try to regain. Intensity. Freshness. Newness. I believe it's what Wordsworth was thinking about when he wrote:

There was a time when meadow, grove, and stream,
The earth, and every common sight
To me did seem
Apparell'd in celestial light,
The glory and the freshness of a dream.
It is not now as it hath been of yore; –
Turn wheresoe'er I may,
By night or day,
The things which I have seen I now can see no more.

The Romantic poets were not alone in their fascination with subjective intensity and innocence. Modernists and postmodernists were inspired by the art of children, naive art, outsider art and the art produced in mental asylums. Shakespeare and Beckett entrusted their wise fools with the freedoms of childlike disinhibition. What these characters say is arresting, intuitive – it's worth hearing.

Be curious and be open to wonder. The attentiveness required for creative writing may release the part of you that is unjaded, that can be bothered, that hasn't seen-it-all-done-it-all before. Can it keep you young? There's a memorable bit of graffiti on a wall in east London that says: *it's never too late to have a happy childhood.*

71
LOSE YOURSELF

I don't want time to fly. Time is precious, to be relished. I wish there could be more of it. Life ends, and then there is no time. Even so, there are certain enjoyable activities that make time fly in the most moment-relishing way. They demand observation, concentration, imagination and skilful making. Creative writing is one of those activities. While I write, time is at once super-fast and super-slow.

Creative writing takes me to a different place, away from my worries and woes, a place where I concentrate, where time is concentrated, and yet time can go by so quickly I suddenly realize I haven't left my seat for hours, it's gone dark outside and I haven't even turned the light on.

One Sunday, a friend of mine talked about drawing a boat while she was on holiday. 'You're drawing that boat. The boat becomes you. It's not the same when you take a photo. You spend hours drawing, and you truly observe. Later, when you look back at the drawing, you remember everything, the ants crawling over your toes, and the feeling of sand under your feet.'

The boat becomes you. I love that. I'm reminded of a Buddhist idea that all things are interdependent, interfused and balanced. This is a dynamic surrender of self. The poem becomes you, the scene becomes you, the character becomes you.

When poet-novelist Boris Pasternak portrays a writer immersed in his work, it reads like a description of *flow* (a mental state identified and analyzed by psychologists decades later). His character Zhivago writes out old poems and sketches of poems 'in a flowing hand' before getting into his stride and starting a new poem:

> *Two or three stanzas poured out onto the paper, with a number of images that astonished him. Now his work took possession of him, and he felt close to what people call inspiration. [...] Language, the home and vessel of beauty and sense, itself begins to think and speak on his behalf, and all becomes music, not in the sense of outward, audible sounds but in the sense of the power and impetus of its inner flow.*

The writer is feeling immersed, engaged, fulfilled, without ego. He is part of an irresistible movement forward. And something else happens:

> *He no longer felt like reproaching himself or feeling discontented; the sense of his personal insignificance left him for a time.*

Zhivago's uplifted emotional state – less self-reproach, less discontentment – is in itself inspiring.

Dedicate time to your creative work, open yourself to the power and impetus of that inner musical flow, and heed the positive feelings that draw you back to the sketchbook, back to the studio, back to the computer, or back to the notebook, to lose yourself, again and again.

72

THE PEN IS MIGHTIER THAN THE SWORD

What to do with bullies, racists and predators?

Turn them into material.

Don't cower.

Analyze them.

Cut them down to size.

Box them in.

Disarm them.

Pity them.

Promote a different worldview.

It's the happiest way to win.

73
AN ARGUMENT FOR TRUTH

We know that truth is relative, incomplete, subjective, shifting – and yet we need some anchors to live by. Witnesses in court are asked to tell the whole truth and nothing but the truth. The publishing industry relies on literary genres and marketing categories that plainly differentiate non-fiction from fiction.

Every writer worth their salt will make a claim for truth – especially poets and writers of fiction. In her 1955 essay 'Place in Fiction', writer-teacher Eudora Welty states that art 'is never the voice of a country; it is an even more precious thing, the voice of the individual, doing its best to speak, not comfort of any sort, indeed, but truth.' And which art form excels in truth? 'The art that speaks it most unmistakably, most directly, most variously, most fully, is fiction.'

How can it be that an inventor of fantastical worlds is in the same breath a purveyor of truth? Surely it is the preserve of non-fiction writers, biographers and historians? Now I smile. Even the allegedly impartial language of science and law is written from a point of view, skewed by emotion, political approach and the limits of knowledge.

Try writing two plausible stories from the first-person point of view and set in the past: one, a lived experience, entirely truthful; the other, a wholly fictional tale based on invented and researched information. Can any story be totally truthful? Can any story be totally fictional?

Ours has been called the age of irony, when art comes with a knowing smirk. It is difficult to create art with sincerity. Good creative writing is not necessarily fancy or clever, but true.

What do I mean by 'true'? Novelist and diarist André Gide has a good answer. In his journal of 1891 he notes: 'When one has begun to write, the hardest thing is to be sincere. Essential to mull over that idea and to define artistic sincerity. Meanwhile, I hit upon this: the word must never precede the idea. Or else: the word must always be necessitated by the idea. It must be irresistible and inevitable; and the same is true of the sentence, of the whole work of art.'

Write with authenticity, however you interpret this overused word. Let words come *after* ideas, made necessary by ideas.

Cultivate your emotional truth – even when it chafes. *Not comfort of any sort.*

Truth is the grit needed to make a pearl.

74
PERSON-BUILDING

Out of the blue, I receive an email from a woman who attended my creative writing workshops a year or two before. She merrily confesses that she has not yet written her great novel, or any novel. In fact, she hasn't done any 'creative writing' at all. She wants to tell me something else.

Ever since doing the course, things started changing for her at work. She was writing shorter, better emails, and receiving better responses; client issues were being resolved more quickly and calmly than usual. Her business reports were prompting positive feedback from colleagues. Her manager noticed all of this and gave her a pay rise. Months later, she had a promotion and another pay rise.

Her novel might yet happen, but that's not the big story here.

The good news is that, through the discipline of creative writing, this person communicates more effectively and is better understood. She has developed her self-expression, her empathy with clients and colleagues, her confidence and her capabilities – for which she earns emotional and other rewards.

When cynics assert that to study creative writing is a waste of time, they're assuming that most writing graduates won't write the next literary sensation – and they're right. Most writing graduates won't write the next literary sensation. But that's missing the point.

Writer-teacher George Saunders defends the study of creative writing as beneficial even for the many who don't complete or publish work:

> *The process of trying to say something, of working through craft issues and the worldview issues and the ego issues – all of this is character-building [...] I've seen, time and time again, the way that the process of trying to say something that matters dignifies and improves a person.*

I encourage you to work through the craft issues. Work through the worldview issues. Work through the ego issues. Build, and keep on building.

75
YOUR DIARY WILL KEEP YOU

When I invite you to keep a diary (*Chapter 36*), my assumption is that your uninhibited chronicling has no audience, and the process itself is goal enough. But there may be a different kind of outcome. A bonus, if you like.

'I always say, keep a diary and someday it'll keep you.' So says a screenplay character of actor-writer Mae West. Memoirists before her said something along the same lines, playing with an old proverb about keeping your shop and your shop keeping you. The implicit connection with trading, or doing business, is not incidental here.

Career politicians actively maintain their diaries in a tactical way, hoping some day to make capital out of the material of their daily lives. Narrative structure comes later, along with hindsight and a ripening desire to influence history. Once published, such memoirs depend on the detail of real-time reporting for their vividness and veracity. Others in the public eye – sportspeople, performers and celebrities – do as politicians do: they invest in words today for tomorrow's use.

Nawal El Saadawi's secret childhood diary gave her the opportunity for unconstrained self-expression, exploring her anger at authority and the injustices of patriarchy. Those early explorations kickstarted her brilliant career as writer, physician, psychiatrist, teacher and activist.

A writer-friend of mine kept a diary in his teens. It was a period of extremely testing experiences he couldn't share with anyone. Decades later, he used these writings as inspiration for a beautifully crafted podcast.

I know another writer whose poignant memoir is based, detail by detail, on the journal she wrote as a schoolgirl in the 1960s. She now describes her teenage diary as the therapist that kept her alive, although she didn't know it then.

Dear Diarist, you don't need to have clear-cut motives when you start journalling, but you never know what good material you'll find in your former life once you've got some distance on it.

76
REWRITE HISTORY

When a dear writer-friend became terminally ill and died, I mourned and missed him. And missed him. I found myself making notes about him, trying not to lose vivid details of his life. Eventually, 'he' made his way into the novel I was writing at the time. He's not the protagonist, but he's there, one of a cast of characters in a supporting role. In my story, he doesn't die. He is alive.

This is a small history, one that matters to me.

You can rewrite big history, as Robert Harris did in *Fatherland*, the fiction thriller with an alternative narrative where Nazi Germany has won World War II. Rewriting public history is disruptive. There's something satisfying about Quentin Tarantino's revisionist revenge screenplays: *Inglourious Basterds*, where Jews assassinate Nazi leaders, and *Once Upon a Time in Hollywood*, where the Manson-cult killers don't get to murder anybody, but are themselves brutally dispatched.

One of the freedoms of being a writer is that you can look back at history, private or public, and make a different story with it. You can invent, rewrite, unwrite the past. You know that history is usually written by the victors. Which perspectives will you adopt? From well-informed conjecture to unfettered fantasy, the past is yours to reshape and retell.

Enjoy this freedom.

PS: In some languages, the words for *history* and *story* are one and the same. It is all the telling of tales.

77
INVENT AN ALTERNATIVE PRESENT

Writing can be a way of upgrading the here and now – or trying to. A different narrative can correct, adjust or subdue the disappointments and disgraces of existence. Writers can describe being anywhere, doing anything. We can rewrite life to suit ourselves. We are all Billy Liars.

The alternative present can be a matter of interpretation, where harsh actuality is made more tolerable through reasoning and creativity. In her diary, Anne Frank took control of her time and space by creating her own solitary teenage universe, away from the censure of adults and the horrors of the world outside.

The alternative present can continue a discontinued personal history, as Reg Thompson did in *Dear Charlie: Letters to a Lost Daughter*. This memoir is a collection of heart-breaking correspondence written to a child after her unexpected death. In the book's introduction, he explains 'I began to write to her, talking to her as if she was away on holiday or at boarding school, keeping her up to date with the small events of an ordinary life. Above all I wanted to tell her how much I love her, how much I will always love her. It became and remains an obsession. When I write I am with her, surrounded by her presence, immersed in memories of her.'

The alternative present can be a matter of inventive distortion in order to reveal the dangers of current trends, often invisible to us because we are enmeshed in things as they are. The writer asks: 'What if…?' or, more disturbing still, 'Actually, really, what are we doing?' Satire flourishes here, as does speculative fiction. In his 1729 pamphlet 'A Modest Proposal', Jonathan Swift uses chillingly deadpan prose to expose societal cruelty and hypocrisy. He paints an emotive portrait of the poor in the Ireland of his time, only then to propose a pragmatic solution to the problem: the sale of poor children as meat for the wealthy. Just as off-key is George Saunders' 2012 novella 'The Semplica-Girl Diaries'. Through an aspiring, cheerful everyman narrator, a dark mirror is held to the realities of our time: consumerism, the inequalities of globalization, and the commodification of human beings. Some dehumanizing luxury technology is thrown in for good measure.

The message for today? You've got to accept the way things are – unless, of course, you're a writer. You can rewrite the present with the hope of making things better. And – who knows? – such action may even succeed in making things better.

78

WRITE THE FUTURE

Aldous Huxley and Mary Shelley are just two of the writers we know to have been inspired by scientific discovery to create their extraordinary fictive worlds. But too often we forget how much scientific innovation in the real world actually stems from fiction.

The physicist Robert H. Goddard, credited with ushering in the space age, created and built the world's first liquid-fuelled rocket. What inspired him? A novel he read when he was a teenager: H.G. Wells' *War of the Worlds*. Isaac Asimov's 'Three Laws of Robotics' (introduced in a 1942 short story) are still taken seriously by the AI and robotics industries today. The novel *Ready Player One* inspired the founder of tech giant Oculus VR when he was still in the crowdfunding phase; he handed out the book as 'required reading' to employees. Eliot Peper's article in *Harvard Business Review*, 'Why business leaders need to read more science fiction', argues that science fiction can help us to reframe the world, enabling us to see things from a new perspective. No doubt this is why science fiction writers are hired by firms such as Microsoft, Apple and Google.

Innovation consultant Ezri Carlebach likes to explore 'one of the stranger aspects of being human, that is, our ability to imagine things that don't exist – to reason, as a recent *New Yorker* article put it, about unreasonable things.' This is beyond saying that we humans have imagination.

Certainly, we can imagine hunting scenes and we can paint them from our dreams or memories onto our cave walls. We can even paint our cave walls with invented creatures that are part beast, part human, potentially mystical. But we take it further.

'The point is,' Carlebach continues, 'that because people can imagine things that don't exist, they can – and do – spend hours calculating the azimuth and elevation angles for navigating the USS *Enterprise* through deep space, or debating the relative probability that the ancient god Cthulhu exists as opposed to, say, the Loch Ness monster. They can do this even though they don't truly believe any of those things are real. And not only can they imagine them, they can draw them, paint them, write stories about them and make movies about them – and these are big industries, employing lots of people.'

Speculative writing is not confined to fantasy and science fiction. When a reality-TV personality was elected President of the largest economy on Earth, and later when a comedy-actor who played the role of 'president' on a TV show was elected President of a huge nation-state, readers felt inspired to contact me with messages of amazement at the obliquely prophetic reach of my novel *The TV President*. Decades after publication, real life seemed to be catching up with fiction.

I suspect that such materializations happen to fiction writers all the time. In his essay 'Why Write?', John Updike commented on the frequently prophetic quality of his fictions, to the point where people would appear in his life who'd started out as fictional characters. Reality eventually acts out our imaginings: when we write, we do so out of latency, not just memory.

I obsess about things, I observe, I imagine, I have dreams and nightmares, I feel compelled to write. It may be enough to address an obsession directly. Writing non-fiction gives me satisfaction in a straightforward way. But something quite different happens when I'm creating fiction. Is it writing out of latency? The process feels mysterious, risky, not a matter of literal interpretation so much as lateral exploration. In this sense, perhaps all fiction is speculative fiction.

Here's a powerful future-writing exercise: pretend you've completed your literary work and write a review of it. This is the positive critical review you'd like to receive. The 'critic' might be yourself. A family member or friend. Maybe a stranger – an online reader or professional literary critic. Point out genre, form, themes, style, aesthetic qualities, effect, comparable works, likely audience. Don't be shy of details. Don't refrain from praise – this is more than a synopsis.

Once you've written it, notice how this review makes you think and feel.

Keep it.

Remind yourself to read it now and then.

Write towards making it come true.

The future is yours to write.

79
FIND MATERIAL IN MISFORTUNE

At a literary festival, I heard a crime-fiction writer speaking about a real-life incident when he and a friend were assaulted and held captive during a robbery. It was a violent and terrifying situation. And yet, in the middle of his terror, he was thinking *I'm going to get something out of this.*

I've heard other creatives express similar thoughts.

During some of my toughest times, I've sensed a tiny part of me – perhaps the writer within – observing. With the practice of writing, as with the practice of mindfulness, I've tried to train myself to observe thoughts, feelings, events, rather than be overwhelmed by them.

I do not seek pain in order to fuel my creativity, but life will dish up struggle and hurt anyway. If you're a writer, that struggle and hurt is potentially rich fodder for creative expression. In 1945, Anaïs Nin wrote in a letter that 'great art was born of great terrors, great loneliness, great inhibitions, instabilities, and it always balances them.' I'd lose the word *great*.

80
WRITE OUT THE NEGATIVE

In her 1942 autobiographical work *Dust Tracks on a Road*, author Zora Neale Hurston wrote that 'there is no agony like bearing an untold story inside you.' In recent times, social psychologist and writing therapy pioneer James Pennebaker has researched the links between language, trauma and recovery. Intriguingly, he began by studying the health consequences of holding on to – or disclosing – traumatic secrets. Inspired by his groundbreaking scientific work, professionals in psychology and psychiatry have investigated the effects of 'expressive writing' on various physical symptoms, immune function, post-operative recovery, cancer-related morbidity and so on. Researchers have found that, for many people, writing about their deepest thoughts and feelings can lead to better health – and notably fewer visits to the doctor.

Here's a writing activity inspired by this work. If you find yourself thinking and worrying about something too much, promise yourself to write about it for 15+ minutes daily – but only for three or four days. (The idea is not to write about upheaval on a daily basis forever; this can actually get you stuck in a negative cycle.) Write for yourself, not for anyone else, not to anyone else. Write as you see fit, not as you think you're *supposed* to write. Be open and descriptive. Don't worry about grammar or spelling; corrections can lead to self-censorship. Plan to destroy what you've written – even if you don't. If this writing activity does not feel beneficial for you, do something else. (And if you're concerned about any physical or mental health condition, consult a doctor or other healthcare professional.)

For everyday worries and woes, my personal writing remedy is this: I make a list of the things that are getting me down. The act of writing contains them, manages them, makes some sense of them. It helps me to confront them and recognize them for what they are. Sometimes I'm surprised at how lightweight the list is because it felt so heavy before writing it. Sometimes, once they're itemized, negative experiences or people become less vexing. Writing doesn't take the vexations away, but it does take away some of the sting.

Writing for therapeutic reasons is different from writing for art.

Art involves sublimation. It also involves making, the crafting of ideas and artefact. From alchemy to chemistry to psychoanalysis, the term *sublimation* has always involved transition from one state to another. Deflection. Translation. Transformation.

In her autobiographical essay 'A Sketch of the Past', Virginia Woolf writes that 'a shock is at once in my case followed by the desire to explain it. [...] It is only by putting it into words that I make it whole; this wholeness means that it has lost its power to hurt me; it gives me, perhaps because by doing so I take away the pain, a great delight to put the severed parts together. Perhaps this is the strongest pleasure known to me. It is the rapture I get when in writing I seem to be discovering what belongs to what; making a scene come right; making a character come together.' Here Woolf connects the different pleasures of writing therapeutically and writing artistically. They are both processes of achieving wholeness and coherence.

81
WRITE UP THE POSITIVE

It's reasonable to assume that writers make use of painful experience, but it's not so reasonable to assume that we start out with more-than-average pain. Nor do we need to have extra rations of pain in order to be inspired. Creative writing may be a colourful way of refracting the negative, but it may equally be a celebration of the positive.

Declaration: writing this book is making me feel happy. And well. And resilient. There's a definite spring in my step.

When I was deep into writing my last novel, regardless of the tone of a chapter or scene, I felt a general sense of satisfaction, commitment and purpose, a quiet inner anchoring – even during difficult times.

When I was researching and writing a collection of true stories about finding love, I positively out-smiled the Cheshire Cat. This is an extract from the book's introduction:

> *Other people's happy endings make me feel happy. It was a happy task prompting others to tell their tale. One couple who pounced on the idea said instantly 'recalling how we fell in love makes us*

fall in love all over again.' […] If people who face the world with positive feelings tend to experience more positive events than those who don't, happy endings are better for you than spinach or chocolate.

Just as recalling good times prompted my interviewees to have newly joyful feelings, hearing or reading a happy story can make us feel happier. In creative writing workshops, after sharing positive stories, student-writers observe that the very act of sharing has reinforced the joy, amplifying it and validating it.

Writing about happy things can make you – and others – feel happy.

82
TAKE IT ON THE CHIN

Many people think that criticism is negative, like abuse or insult. But criticism is a positive action.

Offering it is positive because in formulating your thoughtful response to a text you recognize what your views and values are. You make discoveries. If your criticism is constructive, you'll be helping to solve creative problems for another writer and indirectly for yourself too. It's necessary for their craft, and for yours.

Receiving criticism is positive too, despite the fact that it might feel painful. It's no use just hanging out for applause. Get feedback. Join a class, a writers' club or organization, go to pub readathons, network online, enter writing competitions, join crowd-writing projects, send your work to specialists for readers' reports, attend open-mic nights, poetry slams, spoken-word events… Audiences are good for you because they make you do real writing and they give you real responses.

The first lesson to learn is that there is no correct interpretation. You may write with intentions, but you don't consciously know all of them, and nor should you. Truly creative works are in some ways mysterious, even to their creators. You can't dictate meaning, although you can do your best to influence.

Your audience will let you know what they like or don't like. They are entitled to surprise you. They might be describing a hilarious comedy, despite your intention to make them weep at the bleakness of the human condition. Their misinterpretation may hurt, but you can see that it's good for you. Are you funnier than you realized? If so, stick with it, unleash your comedic side, or you may want to reconsider your tragic verbs.

Often there's a literary element that will bother one reader for one reason (say, a matter of accuracy) and another person for an altogether different reason (say, a matter of taste). If this happens, you know that there's a glitch embedded here, even if neither critic has quite identified it.

It may be that the criticism pulls in two different directions – the very quality that one reader likes is problematic for another. You need to listen to the debate, learn to interpret your interpreters, and decide how to edit, not forgetting your creative instinct. You'll get better and better at this the more you expose your work to feedback.

The push-me-pull-you critical effect is likely to happen if you submit your work to agents or publishers, go the self-publishing route or upload your work for any kind of online viewing.

So before going global with distribution, it's good to get the bugs out of the system. Seek out the response of trusted peers and deal with it even when it's difficult, before throwing yourself into stranger danger: agents, publishers, critics and reviewers, the internet community worldwide.

Whatever criticism you receive, be tough, be lovely, be lofty, and take it on the chin. It's good for you. It's good for your chin. As Ignatius of Loyola wrote: 'Laugh and grow strong.'

83

SEE MORE

At art school, my favourite and least favourite days were Tuesdays. Every Tuesday was dedicated to drawing and painting. Life models. Still-life. Reportage. We were tasked with representing what we saw to best effect using a specific medium (crayon, charcoal, graphite pencil, oil paint, gouache, watercolour…). It sounds easy, doesn't it? Think of all those artworks with five lines where one will do. A few lines here, a head there, some legs there and bingo: you have a picture of a human.

But if you look, if you *really* look, legs don't do what legs should do. Light and shadow behave in determinedly unrealistic ways – and they change from one moment to the next. Perspective distorts the most predictable of lines. You end up drawing horizontals where verticals should be, curves instead of straight lines. You see purple where you expected beige. You must decide which of this landscape's infinite details you will bring to the fore, and which you will suppress.

You have to look, *really* look.

'Build up the scene with the background first. Use the white of the paper underneath,' said one teacher. 'The paper's white is one of your colours. Make the most of watercolour's transparency.' (This is like using silence as an instrument in music or storytelling.)

'Draw without using lines, not one single line,' another teacher said. 'Turn your charcoal on its side and block out light and shade until you create the body's forms. See the subject purely in terms of light and shade.' It felt more natural to make outlines first, to fill them in, to draw what was already in my mind.

I found these challenges difficult (which is why I fretted about art school Tuesdays) and very exciting (which is why I loved art school Tuesdays). They taught me to see differently – better, more keenly – forever.

It's not easy to drop a habit, especially if that habit is a way of seeing. Whether it's prose or poetry, good writing is about perceiving, really perceiving. It's easy to be seduced by the comfort of convention. It's easy to write 'the scent of tulips' because it sounds pretty in a romantic poem, but what do tulips smell of, actually?

When Tracy Chevalier's character Vermeer asks his servant-girl with the pearl earring to identify the colour of the clouds, her first response is to say 'white'. He corrects her. She looks, properly. She sees yellow, then blue and grey. She sees colours in the clouds, as Vermeer does.

Here's a deceptively simple exercise: try describing the sky. (The potential for cliché is great – how many times has a sky been described?) First, I invite you to look at the sky, as if for the first time. Notice what you notice. Use your own words to convey what you see, as you see it. Let the meaning come first, then choose the words to fit the meaning most exactly.

Once you have written your description, try depicting this sky from another point of view, say, that of your nine-year-old self, or that of your 99-year-old self. With each of these perspectives, notice what you notice, and what words you use.

If you're happy to continue sky-gazing, try perceiving and writing as another character altogether. Notice what you notice, and what words you use.

There is always the choice of what to bring to the fore, and what to suppress. An artwork, even the most obviously true to life, is nothing if not a matter of interpretation. But within that interpretation there is the truth of perceiving, really perceiving. The artist's gaze, the writer's gaze, must be focused on truth, no matter how subjective. In *A Room of One's Own,* Virginia Woolf writes that 'fiction must stick to facts – and the truer the facts the better the fiction'.

Write with this intensity of gaze. Your writing, and your vision, will get better.

84
ENJOY MORE BRAIN POWER

When we take notes at a lecture, we recall more of the important information and ideas than if we simply listen without taking notes. As we put pen to paper, we organize, evaluate and decide what to record. We make concepts of our own. This kind of note-taking helps us learn better and remember more. Interestingly, research shows that if we write by hand, we remember more than if we type.

When we write about an activity, our brains fire up as if ready to perform that activity. Focused visualizing can improve our recall and even our real-life performance of certain skills. When we write, the connections made between different neural regions help to strengthen our retention of information. As we brainstorm, and as we create stories, we improve our memory fitness because we're actively engaging with information, we contextualize it, we concentrate, we make links and see relevance between disparate things, and we repeat the reinforcing processes of retrieval.

Memory – and memories – are the creative writer's bread and butter.

There's the objective material, fixed facts and figures, records and transcriptions, word-for-word quotations... If you write these down attentively, you're more likely to remember them. Keep your notebook active. Make notes. And more notes.

Then there's the subjective material: stories, people, places, experiences, dreams, ideas, sensations...

Right now I can recall my grandmother's laugh. She died long ago, and there is no recording of her voice that I know of, but I can hear her in my mind's ear. This is an imaginative reconstruction; it may even be an act of construction. Each time I remember my grandmother's laugh I am a different person – I am older, more or less sentimental, and so on. My relationship to my memory changes too. It may be that I am having a memory of a memory of a memory and, like a copy of a copy of a copy, each impression loses some of the original's exact quality.

But if I choose to sit down and write about my grandmother's laugh, I'm sure to find that the act of writing opens up recollections that are not degraded copies. I'll remember long-forgotten experiences, possibly for the first time. It's as if a portal opens and an archival store is suddenly, newly, released in all its fresh and particular detail. The very act of writing is a catalyst for remembering. I'm not alone in this – ask Marcel Proust, or any memoirist. From retention to retrieval, creative writing helps you to remember well.

But that's not all. Writing makes you smarter in other ways.

In the act of writing, ideas come to light and gain definition.

Writing well means better, sharper observation.

Writing well means better, sharper interpretation.

Writing well is thinking well.

Write – and enjoy more brain power.

85
MAKE YOURSELF FEEL

Gustave Flaubert was probably working on *Madame Bovary* when he wrote in a letter: 'I had to get up and fetch my handkerchief; tears were streaming down my face. I had been moved by my own writing: the emotion I had conceived, the phrase that rendered it, and the satisfaction of having found the phrase – all were causing me the most exquisite pleasure.'

Unexpected emotional connections may happen when you give time to creative writing. You tap into feelings you didn't consciously recognize within you before starting to write. You might discover, or rediscover, love. You might unearth forgotten desires. You might find release for suppressed disappointment. You might realize you're confronting an unpleasantness you would normally avoid. You might start crying about something quite mysterious.

If you're yawning with boredom as you write, chances are that your reader will be bored too, and you'd do well to refresh your palette, or wake up your body, or call it a day. You need to care about your subject matter and your craft. If you're writing without empathy for your characters, your reader is unlikely to feel very much for them. There's no guarantee that compassion in your work will induce compassion in your reader, but it's more likely to do so than authorial indifference.

The cathartic element may remain evident in the finished artefact of your making, or you may write through it and out to the other side where it is metamorphosed into something new, beyond easy recognition. Either way, feeling is a route to creating something aesthetic, which is the opposite of anaesthetic.

Write to make yourself feel.

86
FEEL WITH OTHERS

Philosopher Jason Baehr reasons that curiosity, attentiveness and open-mindedness are intellectual virtues needed for good thinking and learning. Clinical psychologist Simon Baron-Cohen suggests that interpersonal problems, from neighbourly disputes to international conflicts, can be dissolved with empathy. Compassionate empathy connects you with others without being emotionally overwhelmed. Empathy fuels better social connections and helpful behaviours that are of benefit to everyone.

As a creative writer, you constantly need to put on other people's hats and wear their shoes – metaphorically speaking. If you properly imagine how the world looks and feels from other perspectives, you're using your powers of empathy. A friend of mine calls this process *novelizing*, even when novels have nothing to do with it. It's externalizing in the most positive sense: not distancing, but the opposite. Inhabiting the other's imaginative space. Getting inside their head. Getting outside your own head.

You're novelizing when you get past ventriloquism. When your writing embodies authentic voices beyond your own. When your characters are not all the same. When you craft communications for an organization, thinking carefully about their audience's wants and needs, rather than pushing some corporate process or belief. When you seek understanding about your own story as a life lived with others, different people connecting and disconnecting, cooperating and clashing.

If you're not getting to the heart of a character and you're writing in the third person, try rewriting their story in the first person. This process is especially helpful if the character is hateful or alien to you. The moment you write from the perspective of *me, myself* and *I*, compelling new details will emerge, and you'll know what to investigate more fully. You'll be feeling *with*, not looking *at*. (You can always revert to the third person afterwards.)

Apply yourself to the practice of creative writing on a regular basis, and you're novelizing most of the time. If, as Aristotle suggested, you are what you repeatedly do, you're generally building your powers of empathy while you're crafting words, imagining scenes, observing real people, being curious about their motivation and behaviour. The more you write, and the more you read, the better you get at putting on other hats and stepping into other shoes. Even when they don't fit. Especially when they don't fit.

Here's an exercise in antipathy, sympathy, empathy.

Write a portrait of a character whom the narrator dislikes. Build up the picture so that we too feel negative about this character, perhaps in subtle ways, perhaps in obvious, extreme ways. Consider the implicit point of view. Who is creating this portrait? What is implied about the narrator's relationship with their subject? What stories have happened between them? What are the reasons for the narrator's negativity? Make sure we share the narrator's feelings.

Write a portrait of exactly the same character, but with sympathy and positive feelings. This portrait should not be a mere contradiction of the first portrait, not a simple good-for-bad swap. This portrait should offer complex and revealing new insights into the character we thought we knew and disliked. Again, whose point of view is implied by the writing? What relationships and events emerge? Turn our feelings around.

The two portraits should together make a satisfying short story or poem, not just a two-way description. Think about structure, the process of revelation, the subjectivity of truth.

87 REMEMBER THE OTHER DOG'S BONE

One of Aesop's fables is a story that comes to my mind quite often. I'll tell it the way I remember it.

There's a dog with a nice, juicy bone in his mouth. As he crosses a bridge over a stream, he looks down and sees another dog with what looks like a larger, juicier bone between his teeth. The dog on the bridge snaps at the other dog to grab the bigger bone. He drops his own. When it falls into the water, the reflection is shattered. There is no other dog. There is no bigger, juicier bone. The dog on the bridge is left with no bone at all.

Some writers, acclaimed or struggling, torture themselves with feelings of failure and the curse of competitive comparison. Remember the other dog's bone when you worry about measuring your success as a writer against others.

Remember the other dog's bone just anyway.

88
PERSEVERANCE WORKS

Painter-printmaker Katsushika Hokusai, who in his early seventies created *The Great Wave off Kanagawa*, wrote that nothing he drew before the age of 70 was notable, and he hoped to make real progress by the time he got to 80. When he died at the age of 89, he said that he might manage to become a true artist if he had five more years.

An elderly writer-friend of mine was fortunate enough to be taught by Martha Foley, the activist and co-founder of *Story* magazine, who is credited with launching the careers of Tennessee Williams, J.D. Salinger, Truman Capote, Carson McCullers and others.

My friend said that, at the end of the last creative writing class, Ms Foley asked her students if they wanted to know the secret to success.

Of course they did.

'Yes,' they answered as one, impatient, keen.

With great solemnity, she picked up her chalk, turned to the blackboard and wrote, very slowly, in huge capital letters: PERSEVERANCE.

Like cycling, dentistry, singing, juggling – most things – writing improves with deliberate, dedicated practice.

The more you paint, the more skilful you become at observing, choosing and preparing your materials, mixing and combining colours, exploiting the properties of the medium, handling brushes and other tools, playing with techniques, composing, creating images, transforming concepts into expressive artefact.

Likewise, with the practice of creative writing.

Stick with it, and you'll become skilful at observing, choosing and preparing your material, combining perspectives and styles, exploiting the properties of genre, handling words, playing with techniques, composing, creating images, transforming concepts into expressive artefact. You'll resolve your technical weaknesses and develop your strengths. You'll develop your unique voice.

Start. Stick at it. Follow it through until it works.

89
GOALS, GOALS, GOALS

'I'm playing at a serious concert in November,' a friend tells me. 'My diary until then is a big banana.'

She's a harpist, but she's not a professional musician. She's nervous because she's never performed the chosen work before, and it involves a notoriously difficult solo. She wants to do it well. There are six months to go. Meanwhile, there's the day-job.

But what is the diary banana?

'A curve towards that month,' she says. Her hand makes an arc in the air, from here to there. From now to then.

I like my friend's attitude. She's making herself do something she can't already do – a new piece, a difficult piece. She is focusing her energy towards the date when she will have to play to a paying public, and she wants to do it well: for herself, for the orchestra, for the audience.

Actually, I'm writing about this in the present tense, but the concert has happened. She performed brilliantly. The response was wonderful. She radiated joy.

Have a writing goal. Work towards it. Whatever you need to do in the everyday, you can still follow the diary banana that curves from here to there.

Your goal doesn't need to be a deadline. It might be about attaining skills, or output, or attitude. If you want something enough, you'll do what is needed. It might even be about defining intent, like saying: *I am, or I will be, a writer.* Attempt things you can't do because, by doing, you'll get closer to being able to do them. Start small. Step by step. Piece by piece.

My tai chi teacher says *qi follows yi*: energy follows mind. If you think towards your goal, your energies – and other people's energies too – will be directed towards it. Every decision you make will contribute towards it. Even if you don't achieve your ultimate goal, you'll be further ahead than if you didn't have the goal in the first place.

90

A WRITER'S LIFE IS EASY

There is nothing to writing. All you do is sit down at a typewriter and bleed. This statement in various forms is attributed to Ernest Hemingway, a couple of sports writers and other wordsmiths besides. The idea has clearly hit home.

If the act of writing is itself hard, then surely a writer's life is hard? Yes, it's hard. It's not lying about on cushions picking words like chocolates from a box. It's hard to think, really think. It's hard to compose. It's hard to edit. It's hard if your writing is rejected or ignored. It's hard to navigate your own subjectivity: *I'm writing drivel / I'm writing a work of greatness / Why am I writing at all?*

But it's not hard like battling catastrophic weather events or working in a war zone. Besides, nobody is making you do it. If it's too onerous, do something else.

You can hear it: I'm not very sympathetic when writers complain about how hard it is being a writer.

I was amused to hear novelist Richard Ford in conversation at a literary festival, advising writers to work hard – at making life *not* like being a banker or a lawyer. It's enough to write something and quit, to be happy about whatever you've written that day. Other writers suggest that it's enough to give it a small parcel of time, or write a modest number of words, each day. No hair-shirts, and no treadmills. Fragments. Little and often. Eventually you will reach critical mass.

Forget all those tips about adhering to a strict life-denying routine, or filling timesheets with your epic writing hours. (Unless, of course, these are exactly what you need.) Resist all those dramatic statements about flesh in the inkpot and blood on the keyboard.

Nobody is making you write. You're writing because you want to do it. It's a rewarding practice that requires patience and effort. Accept this, get on with it, and life will actually be much easier.

91
ALL CREATIVITY IS GOOD FOR YOU

Creativity doesn't have to be big or glamorous. It can be a matter of hoarding broken bits and pieces in the hope of creating something new. It can be choosing to make things instead of buying them ready-made. It can be noodling or doodling.

Making is a happy compulsion, an urge. Perhaps you have this compulsion. These student-writers do…

Louise says that creative pursuits tend to be neglected in an otherwise balanced life of work, relationships, exercise and relaxation. When creativity is included in the schedule, she regards it as an essential form of self-care.

Hetian says that creative writing is infinite, there are no limits. Whether he's working through something problematic, or just playing, he feels better after writing: peace, happiness, fulfilment.

Tracey says: 'Creative writing has been hugely liberating for me, from the shy beginnings of letting another person read my work, to learning how to receive feedback, and to slowly, carefully, finding my voice. Not the one I use in work, restricted by the language of the office, but a voice that is my own. I genuinely feel that through writing I've got to know myself better and have found immense enjoyment through bringing new worlds to life.'

These are spontaneous observations based on personal experience, and I concur with them all.

Anecdotal evidence aside, scientific studies reliably show that creativity can promote mental and physical health, from the calming effects of meditative focus to the motivating dopamine-release that occurs when creating a thing: an artwork, a model, a jacket, a cake, a piece of furniture, a dance, a garden, a story... Science also tells us that writing can enhance brain performance: learning, memorization and cognitive functioning. Expressive writing can boost immunity, recovery from trauma and the processing of negative emotions.

But the positive effects of creative endeavour can go far beyond the individual.

Polymath Nawal El Saadawi teaches 'Creativity and Dissidence' courses with the view that conventional education tends to compartmentalize reality – splitting, say, religion, gender, medicine, history – whereas creativity is to unite, to make links. Creative thinking, the unlearning of indoctrination, helps women and men start to know their rights.

Writer-maker John-Paul Flintoff argues that 'when we engage creatively with the world, we are having an impact. Our work can lighten hearts, console, and give people a reason to think of life as something to savour rather than just endure. Works of art (in this widest sense) are ways of building a meaningful community.'

Indulge your urge to create. Make time for making.

Absorption, expressiveness, freedom, fun, purpose, community – all in all, the practice of creative writing can be good for your physical health, your mental health and your political health too.

Spin straw into gold

Folk tales are deceptively simple. They explore big ideas that matter. Love, loss, danger, mystery, cruelty, learning, revenge, justice, conflict, power, hope, ambition, rejection, order, insecurity, death, survival. The stories are reduced and polished through telling and retelling. Locked into few words, and few characters, are all the key elements of good, compelling narrative.

If you are writing a long work, navigating through an excess of material can lead to plot troubles. Interesting characters and incidents can lead you astray if you're not sure of the main path. Both writer and reader may end up being lost in the woods.

Your creative quest: write a complete story as if it were a simple folk tale. The language must be basic. Only essential details are told. Only vital characters are included. The protagonist is distinctive in some way. By the end of the story, a clearly identified challenge is resolved, or a transforming journey is completed.

92
REJOICE: YOU MADE IT

Plato's idea that all art is imperfect and incomplete rests on the notion that there is some impossible and absolute beauty that we can only seek to represent. Our art will always fall short of perfection.

Take a look at the complete works of Geoffrey Chaucer – they're nearly all incomplete. Peep inside the attic of Leonardo da Vinci, another brilliant non-finisher. Creatives tend to amass fragments, scraps, junk, abandoned projects, notebooks, half-finished things. This is the way it should be. It's the nature of the creative process. There's pleasure in trying, and it's liberating just to play.

So how important is it to finish a project?

Finishing is important if it's important for you to finish.

But when is any creative work finished? You get some sense of completion if you've polished a work to the best of your abilities, and there is a physical object to perceive, such as a bound book, or an artwork on show, or a film that has gone all the way through post-production. And yet every creative project can be tinkered with endlessly.

An artefact is really a moment, a pause in the process of making. The object itself is a venturing forth. The reader, the critic, the viewer – each perceiver finishes the work and, with any luck, the conversation keeps going.

Even so, within the constant fluidity of experience, it is satisfyingly solid to mark a moment and say *I made this thing*.

I decorated my birdy bower with these well-chosen sticks and colourful objects.

I rolled this beautiful ball of dung.

I wrote this.

Innumerable writers have said that they don't like to write, but they love having written. Never mind the effort of composition, this is the joy of accomplishment, completion, the pleasure you feel when you finish making a thing.

Flick through an old notebook and see if there's something that catches your magpie eye, an idea that still interests you, a few beautiful stranded words, or the start of a poem. Delve into it. See if you can 'complete' it.

93

IS IT PUBLISHABLE?

Writers usually ask this question when they've been working on a literary project for a long time. What they're really asking is a question about quality and outcome, with lashings of self-doubt: *is it any good?* or *is it worth persevering?*

What to do? Take a break until the creative cravings are irresistible. Remember why you write. Ponder what it means to be publishable.

These answers contain some reassurance for me:

1. Digital technology means that anything and everything is publishable.

2. Who knows what's publishable? Lots of experts – agents and publishers – turned down J.K. Rowling's *Harry Potter*. William Golding's *Lord of the Flies* was rejected 20 times before someone decided it was publishable.

3. Publishability is not the same as quality, or worth. Vincent van Gogh sold painfully few paintings in his life, and those few sales

were thanks to his uncle and brother. Later, his paintings broke global sales records. Many literary bestsellers of Van Gogh's era are books we haven't heard of today – presumably they're not publishable now.

4. Every published writer I know has a stash of rejections to their name.

5. Publishers, agents and authors all agree that it's a gamble. Literary agent Jonny Geller, in his TEDxOxford talk about bestsellers, describes the more-than-publishable work that has the perfect edit, the perfect jacket, the perfect PR, ringing endorsements from reviewers and salespeople, the wholehearted support of bookshops – whereupon the book doesn't sell.

6. *The Da Vinci Code* was more than publishable. Most of Virginia Woolf's works were deemed not publishable.

7. Timing, timing, timing. Your work lands on a publisher's desk just when they are looking for something like your work. Eureka – it's publishable.

8. Timing, timing, timing. Your work lands on a publisher's desk the day after they signed up something like your work. Damn – it's unpublishable.

9. Think hard, research well, write well, read well, keep at it, seek and heed informed critical feedback, focus, edit, polish. Repeat all steps. Then your work will be more or less publishable. And you will be more or less happy, knowing that you have given it your best.

10. Don't get the desire to write confused with the desire to be published.

94

NO NEED TO MAKE MONEY

To make art is not to make money.

Unless you're a professional hack, writing is one of those careers or hobbies that you pursue *not for the money*. You might make a bit of cash from it here or there – a pea-sized advance or a competition prize win – but you don't go authoring for the financial returns. Writing is rewarding in other ways: spiritually, intellectually, emotionally. Like voluntary work. Which is unpaid. Or care work. Which is low-paid.

What of those superstar advances you read about in the news? Those crazy publishers' auctions? Those million-dollar bestsellers? Well, they make the news because they are big or rare events. Like a giant mutant carrot, or a pizza as long as a street.

The Society of Authors regularly publishes the data on average writerly earnings, and they compare unfavourably with the dole, even though writing is a form of employment.

This lack of money, or expectation of it, is wildly liberating. Just think: no pressure to earn. You can be true to your art. No need to keep up with the Joneses. No conversations about 'net worth'. No need to hire staff who can clean the chandelier to your satisfaction. No chandelier.

95
FIND NEW FRIENDS

Dogs are dazzlingly efficient masters of connectivity. Strangers strike up conversation on the flimsiest of pretexts: *How do you get his coat so shiny? Mine are called Fred and Ginger. Does she chase squirrels?* Despite the solitariness of the writer (lonely as a cloud, and so on), writing is as sociable as dog walking.

Go to a party.

'And what do you do?' a stranger asks, eyes dull with habit and politeness.

'I'm mostly a writer.'

'What, like books?' A flicker of scepticism, anticipating a negative.

'I have various jobs but, yes, I write books.'

Within minutes, the stranger is striving to become a character in one of your stories. They try to be interesting, which is more interesting than people who can't be bothered. They confide in you, conferring upon you the humbling privileges of friend and counsellor. They volunteer stories that might be good material. All in all, they *give*.

Contrast this with, say, the medic's experience. When you go to a party and reveal that you're a nurse or a doctor, strangers attempt to use you: 'I have this pain in my neck, and…' They try to get your services for free, without an appointment. All in all, they *take*.

But who needs parties? Or dogs? Beyond peer groups and professional networks, creative writers can talk to anyone, anywhere, about anything, any time.

I'm on a research trip; I have the confidence to approach people I would never otherwise get to know, and ask whatever question I need to ask, from plumbing to politics. I'm deep into a poetic passage about mushrooms, so I have licence to forage with experts. I'm writing a book of happy endings; moments after meeting, strangers in public places are disclosing intimacies or handing over long-treasured love letters. By chance I meet travellers from a place I need to research. Months later, they offer me board, lodging and a tour of their city. Twenty years later, they're still my dear friends.

Creative writing breaks the ice, opens up conversation and unleashes friendships.

96
LOVE YOUR WRITING GROUP

Oddly enough, a positive outcome of your solitary creative writing practice may be an intentional community. If you don't have a writing group already, I recommend joining one, or starting one.

There are writers who seem to create and hone fine literary works on their own but they're usually kept afloat by others, an indulgent spouse or relative, possibly a colleague.

Your writing group is less random, and more sustainable.

First and foremost, you don't have to share a bed, home or workplace with them. People who love you will say you've written a faultless work of genius – which is useless. You need informed, constructive, challenging criticism. Alternatively, you may find that you like each other less once they've had a go at your writing – which is sad. Services rendered can equate to other tasks on the home front: they've read your work, and what a chore that was; now you have to mow the lawn forever.

Contrast this with your writing group: you get together because you write, not because you have feelings for each other – apart from a strong sense of team spirit. You can discuss your work in progress without the pressures of conditional love, approval or payback. They're better able to help you with your scribbling because they do this scribbling thing too. But they're not just writing practitioners. They're readers, editors and critics. They act as forum and research group too. They offer you peer recognition, regardless of the world beyond. And they reliably help you navigate a steady course through emotional waves – those phases when you believe you're writing a masterpiece and/or piece of rubbish.

Then everyone goes back to their own lives and loves.

Over time, incidentally, you may grow to care about each other. You might even become close friends. But, because of how your community began, the writing always comes first.

I love my writing group. Love yours.

97
MAKE RIPPLES

You don't have to be writing about an issue for your words to provoke change. Virginia Woolf quips in *Orlando* that 'a silly song of Shakespeare's has done more for the poor and the wicked than all the preachers and philanthropists in the world'. Abraham Lincoln, Sigmund Freud, Karl Marx, Nelson Mandela and other influential figures have leaned on Shakespeare's *Comedies, Histories & Tragedies* for pragmatic insight and inspiration. The playwright himself would be amazed at a world that has such people in it.

When Jenny Joseph wrote her poem 'Warning', she could hardly have anticipated the formation of an international friendship organization of more than 35,000 women inspired by the poet's idea of growing old disgracefully.

E.B. White, the pig-farming author of *Charlotte's Web*, could not have foreseen the rise in vegetarianism prompted by the predicament of his fictional pig called Wilbur.

Educators, parents, librarians and booksellers across the world have lauded J.K. Rowling's *Harry Potter* novels for triggering a cultural revolution or two: a generation of converts to reading, including hard-to-reach boys, and a revival in the learning of Latin. The UK's culture industry has had multiple *Harry Potter* boosts: travel and tourism, design and retailing, a flourishing UK film industry.

These are newsworthy stories, but it's not just giants and bestsellers that make an impact. Consider the existentialist notion of *committed literature*. The author cannot be non-committal. You take responsibility for the act of creative writing. You take responsibility for the form, and you take responsibility for the content.

Your literary work, no matter how modest, sets off ripples of influence. A decrease of pain, perhaps. An increase in pleasure. A new understanding. Inspiration. A sense of community. Who knows how far those ripples will go?

98
CHANGE THE WORLD

Creative writing can have unintended consequences, indirect reactions and chain reactions, but what if you set out intending to make the world a better place?

Unpacking the idea of bearing witness, John-Paul Flintoff suggests that 'we can change the world both by passing on news about things that need fixing, and by helping promote other people's attempts to fix those things.'

You can make a positive difference through your words, directly addressing the issues that matter most to you – and why not?

Environmental damage, conflict, injustice, terrorism, oppression, suffering… Instead of submitting to helpless inertia or despondency in response to the world's bleak news, you can use your writing skills to effect change. To elucidate the past. To improve the current situation. To prevent the worst from happening in the future. But it's not enough to rant and rail. The more artfully you write as witness, polemicist or activist, the more effective your messaging will be.

What rights would Mary Wollstonecraft champion if she were alive today, and what literary form would she favour? How would Edward Said frame the east-west debate now? What sort of Hope Speech would Harvey Milk compose if he were still alive? Mahatma Gandhi's *Collected Works* include essays, autobiographies, letters and political tracts in about a hundred volumes. What writings would he produce today, and would he take to social media?

Nature writer Rachel Carson combined scientific research with evocative poetic language in *Silent Spring*, a literary work that prompted governments to review, control or ban the use of DDT and other widely used 'biocides'. This publishing phenomenon inspired international changes in public opinion, activism, scientific practice, the chemical industry – and has contributed to better human health.

In more recent times, thoughtfully choosing her subject, her medium and her words, Greta Thunberg spearheaded a global movement of young people to challenge inactivity in the face of climate crisis. Her influence depends on her skilful writing (speeches first, publications later) as much as her commitment. She lives and breathes the Dalai Lama's line: *If you think you are too small to make a difference, try sleeping with a mosquito.*

Choose your subject. Know it. Research it. Care about it.

Choose your form. Public speech. Campaigning letter. Email. Blog. Vlog. Essay. Article. Petition. Slogan. Song. Libretto. Fiction. Non-fiction. Creative non-fiction. Play. Screenplay. Script. Social media. Poetry. Spoken word. Podcast. Pamphlet. Protest banner. Newsletter. Zine.

Choose your words. Use your creativity and your craft, the guidance throughout this book, to engage and persuade, without forgetting the golden rule: to think properly about your audience's wants and needs.

Write the change you wish to see in the world.

99
THE POWER OF EVERYTHING

Be interested in everything.

Read everything.

Learn something from everything.

100
WRITE NOW

Now is the beginning of the future. The quality of your now affects the quality of all your future nows. Now is the most important time of all.

SOME HAPPY STORIES

I cannot resist telling you
some happy stories that
seem to have been prompted
by creative writing.

I

Claire joins my beginners' creative writing course. She's never written *stories* before, just the usual documents and reports expected at work. She's a corporate HR director, a wife and a mother. Over the term, she tries on different writing hats. The results are mixed, but she's not fixated on outcomes. She enjoys the creative process, and goes on to take the next-level course.

Claire starts writing about her childhood. Tentatively at first. She was adopted. Put on a BOAC plane with other abandoned infant girls, and flown from Hong Kong to Britain in the care of flight attendants. Baby Claire was on a plane in 1962.

She writes the story from the third-person point of view. It goes in and out of focus. Significant scenes tend to occur off the page. Week after week, we feel that we are circling the heart of the tale, urging the author to turn that afterthought into a chapter, to explore the emotion behind that memory. Claire worries that it isn't interesting.

One week, she turns up to class with her reworking of the story, now written in the first person. She starts to read. The narrative is utterly transformed. It is brave and beautiful and emotive and truthful. We are all enthralled by the story and want to hear more. It's the beginning of a full-length memoir. It has to be.

But there are gaps. Claire needs to research the who, what, where and when of so-called objective history to inform her personal subjective history. She uses internet searches and social media to get in touch with other adoptees. She attends conferences and reunions.

A few years later, as a result of her writing and researching, Claire has found out about her extended Chinese family, her adoptive family, and her own life; she has unearthed long-lost memories and solved long-lived mysteries; she has made new friends, and paid tribute to her loving parents, including the untold story of her adoptive father, a street urchin whose life was exchanged for a laundry. She shared her writing with him before he died – to his enormous pride. She has done interviews with national radio and newspapers, and participated in the TV programme *Long Lost Family*. She has contributed to the British Chinese Adoption Study, a book that launched government and institutional debate about transracial adoption in the UK, and she has met more than 60 other adoptees, many of whom are beginning to share their own stories. Oh, and Claire has found her writing voice as a blogger.

II

Chris is an accountant. It pays the bills and employment is reliable, but he has no love for it, and little aptitude. The closest he gets to creative writing: the formal emails he must write to clients, signed off with officially kind regards. He comes to class wearing a business suit.

He takes to this new creative writing skill like a natural-born comedian. Every week he gets the rest of us into happy mode. Even the most tragic of assignments turns funny, even the most earnest of his classmates can't help but smile.

Chris is an exemplary student-writer: he turns up every week and applies himself to the homework in between. He responds well to criticism too, so he irons out the bad wrinkles in his writing, keeps the good ones, and learns to know the difference.

After the summer break and halfway through a new intensive course, working up film script ideas, he shares his good news. In fact, before the news, I should have noticed that he's not wearing a business suit any more. He's wearing jeans.

The BBC was looking for talent to discover and develop. Chris responded to an open call for applications. He had a portfolio of work to submit because he'd done all those creative writing assignments and polished his work after thinking through the feedback. He was called in for an interview. He was offered a six-month contract.

Chris emails me: *I love it and can't quite believe it – I still pinch myself when I stand outside Television Centre.*

After his stint developing ideas for new TV shows at the BBC, Chris goes freelance as a comedy entertainment producer, working with the likes of ITV, Channel 4 and the BBC, creating scripts, sketches and treatments for new programmes. This career he loves.

In an email he says: *I hated being an accountant and as a result was terrible at it, but just about got by. Without your course I don't think there's a chance I'd be working in TV. It gave me the skills and confidence I needed. It made me realize that I could be creative.*

III

Kati and Vilmos agree to be interviewed for *The Book of Happy Endings*. I go to their apartment. Honestly, patiently, generously they tell me the story of how they met and fell in love. We sit together for hours. I scrawl pages and pages of notes. I don't know yet what will be useful, what will be vital, what will be incidental. And I don't know where to begin their story, but I know it needs to be from *his* point of view.

> *Vilmos arrived at Victoria Station. He had travelled by train, and train, and ferry, and train, all the way from Hungary. It was 1963. He was nineteen years old, and ready for the world. He was wearing pointed shoes, a suit with a tightly knotted tie, a jaunty hat with a feather in it. He couldn't speak English. London crashed upon him with its fabulous populous clutter. He'd never felt anything like it. He had never been anywhere before, only*

small places, poor places. Places emptied of Jews.
Places porous enough to absorb Jews.

'Hungarian Kiss' is my version of the story that Vilmos and Kati told me. I drew a thread from the huge tangle of information – facts, details, memories and photos. Here is a young man who falls in love with his uncle's wife. There are two words for *kiss* in Hungarian: *puszi* (affectionate, unromantic) and *csok* (the desirous kiss of lovers). My story tells of how *puszi* became *csok*. There are so many taboos here: family ties and expectations, age difference, you name it.

The two became a couple and, more than 40 years later, they are still together – faithful, devoted, inseparable, unmarried.

> *'And here comes the age difference,' Kati smiles. 'I am nearly eighty-two years old and Vilmos is sixty-two. My priorities are different.'*
>
> *Vilmos can dash about London on a bicycle but Kati has felt the physical frailty of age.*
>
> *'People must have seen and formed an opinion,' she reflects. 'And not necessarily the kindest. But when you think about our life, our romance was almost inevitable.'*
>
> *'It has been a gradual process,' says Vilmos. 'Gradually increasing. It has never stopped increasing. There's no point talking about me, or her. There's just us.'*

This is happy ending enough. But there is another happy ending to this story. A year or so after the book's publication, I receive an invitation to the couple's place for Sunday lunch.

On the day, their apartment door opens and I see platters of home-made food inside. There are other people here. It's going to be a bigger event than I imagined. More and more people arrive. The apartment fills. We drink bubbly. There is something here to celebrate, but nobody seems to know what. A birthday? An anniversary? Early retirement?

We are called into the living room. It's a bit of a crush. Vilmos clears his throat and begins reading a prepared speech. His eyes are filling with tears. His voice breaks. He stops. He starts again, but he can't continue. So he hands the script to his old family friend, who reads for him.

> *It all started back in November 1963, when an almost-relation of Kati's arrived to these shores with all the inexperience and naiveté of youth… but let us not go there just yet.*
>
> *Fast forward to last year, when Kati and I agreed to have an 'interview' with Elise Valmorbida who was collecting material for her project* The Book of Happy Endings, *a collection of stories about couples who met and fell in love.*
>
> *With almost no trepidation we talked with Elise and laid it all bare. She brought it to life on the printed page. This retelling proved to be a catalyst. A not-so-sudden urge to cap the rather unconventional with something most couples undertake at the beginning of their life together.*
>
> *Whilst ours is no fairytale, I thought it would still be nice to end it with 'they got married and lived happily ever after.'*

SOME READING
(AND VIEWING,
AND LISTENING)

Fuel for Writing

'Why I Write', George Orwell (*Gangrel*, 1946)

Notes sur le cinématographe (Notes on the Cinematographer), Robert Bresson (Gallimard, 1975)

The Man Who Mistook His Wife for a Hat, Oliver Sacks (Summit/Gerald Duckworth, 1985)

Writing Down the Bones, Natalie Goldberg (Shambhala Publications, 1986)

Burn This Book, edited by Toni Morrison (HarperCollins, 2009)

A Room of One's Own, Virginia Woolf (Hogarth Press, 1929)

How to Change the World, John-Paul Flintoff (Macmillan, 2012)

On Writing: A Memoir of the Craft, Stephen King (Scribner, 2000)

The Consolations of Philosophy, Alain de Botton (Hamish Hamilton, 2000)

Poems, Making Poems

'Humility', Mary Oliver (*Felicity*, Penguin, 2015)

'The Thought Fox', Ted Hughes (*The Hawk in the Rain*, Faber & Faber, 1957)

'Not Writing', Jane Kenyon (*Constance*, Graywolf, 1993)

'Recreation', Audre Lorde (*The Black Unicorn*, W.W. Norton, 1978)

'Digging', Seamus Heaney (*Death of a Naturalist*, Faber & Faber, 1966)

'An Obsessive Combination of Ontological Inscape, Trickery and Love', Anne Sexton (1959; *Selected Poems*, Houghton Mifflin, 1988)

Prose-Poem-Prose

The Collected Works of Billy the Kid, Michael Ondaatje (Anansi Press, 1970)

Le Città Invisibili (Invisible Cities), Italo Calvino (Giulio Einaudi, 1972)

The God of Small Things, Arundhati Roy (Random House, 1997)

Plot-Flouting Fiction

The Buddha in the Attic, Julie Otsuka (Alfred A. Knopf, 2011)

The Life and Opinions of Tristram Shandy, Gentleman,
Laurence Sterne (1759–67)

La Jalousie (Jealousy), Alain Robbe-Grillet (Les Éditions de Minuit, 1957)

Finnegans Wake, James Joyce (Faber & Faber, 1939)

Plot-Flouting Film Scripts

Le Quattro Volte (The Four Times), Michelangelo Frammartino (2010)

Sans Soleil (Sunless), Chris Marker (1983)

L'Année Dernière à Marienbad (Last Year in Marienbad),
Alain Robbe-Grillet (1961)

Eraserhead, David Lynch (1977)

Koyaanisqatsi, writing credits – (scenario): Ron Fricke, Godfrey Reggio,
Michael Hoenig, Alton Walpole (1982)

Repurposing

Wide Sargasso Sea, Jean Rhys (André Deutsch/W.W. Norton, 1966)

Jack Maggs, Peter Carey (UQP/Faber & Faber, 1997)

Meursault, Contre-Enquête (The Meursault Investigation), Kamel Daoud
(Éditions Barzakh, 2013)

A Thousand Acres, Jane Smiley (Alfred A. Knopf, 1991)

Unpacking Stories

'Pixar's 22 Rules of Storytelling', Emma Coats @lawnrocket (Twitter, 2011)

The Writer's Journey: Mythic Structure for Writers, Christopher Vogler
(Michael Wiese Productions, 1998)

Into the Woods: How Stories Work and Why We Tell Them, John Yorke (Penguin, 2013)

Listening to Silence

Acte Sans Paroles I (Act Without Words I), Samuel Beckett (Éditions de Minuit, 1957)

Four Quartets, T.S. Eliot (Faber & Faber, 1940–42)

En Attendant Godot (Waiting for Godot), Samuel Beckett (Éditions de Minuit, 1952)

A Book of Silence, Sara Maitland (Granta, 2008)

Randomness

Rhinocéros (Rhinoceros), Eugène Ionesco (Gallimard, 1959)

Alice's Adventures in Wonderland, Lewis Carroll (Macmillan, 1865)

The Complete Nonsense and Other Verse, Edward Lear (1846–1888; Penguin, 2006)

Oblique Strategies, Brian Eno and Peter Schmidt (1975)

Nosefulness

Das Parfum (Perfume), Patrick Süskind (Diogenes, 1985)

Jitterbug Perfume, Tom Robbins (Bantam, 1984)

Joyfulness

'Everyone Sang', Siegfried Sassoon (*Picture Show,* J.B. Peace, 1919; *The War Poems,* Heinemann, 1919)

'How happy is the little Stone', Emily Dickinson (*Poems, Edited by two of her Friends,* Roberts Brothers, 1891)

'Phenomenal Woman', Maya Angelou (*And Still I Rise*, Random House, 1978)

'I Wandered Lonely as a Cloud', William Wordsworth *(Poems, in Two Volumes*, Longman, Hurst, Rees & Orme, 1807)

'Warning', Jenny Joseph (1962; *Rose in the Afternoon*, J.M. Dent, 1974)

'there is nothing purer than that', Rupi Kaur (*Milk and Honey*, Andrews & McMeel, 2015)

'Eternity', William Blake (Notebook, c.1794; *The Complete Poetry and Prose of William Blake*, Doubleday, 1965)

A Midsummer Night's Dream, William Shakespeare (c.1595; first quarto, 1600)

Orlando: A Biography, Virginia Woolf (Hogarth Press, 1928)

Pride and Prejudice, Jane Austen (T. Egerton, 1813)

The Diary of a Nobody, George and Weedon Grossmith (J.W. Arrowsmith, 1892)

Three Men in a Boat, Jerome K. Jerome (J.W. Arrowsmith, 1889)

Cold Comfort Farm, Stella Gibbons (Longman, 1932)

Bibliotherapy

Staying Alive: Real Poems for Unreal Times, Neil Astley (Bloodaxe, 2002)

The Novel Cure: An A to Z of Literary Remedies, Ella Berthoud and Susan Elderkin (Canongate, 2013)

The Poetry Pharmacy: Tried-and-True Prescriptions for the Heart, Mind and Soul, William Sieghart (Particular Books, 2017)

REFERENCES

1
WHY WRITE?

—Page 13 extract is from *Why I Write* by George Orwell 1946, © the Estate of Sonia Brownell Orwell 1984. Published by Penguin Books 2004. Reproduced by permission of Penguin Books Ltd. © *Why I Write* by George Orwell (Copyright © George Orwell, 1946) Reprinted by permission of Bill Hamilton as the Literary Executor of the Estate of the Late Sonia Brownell Orwell

4
SHORT IS SWEET

—Translation of Catullus by Nadia Valmorbida and Elise Valmorbida

—Translation of Matsuo Bashō by Katsura Isobe and Elise Valmorbida

9
INDULGE YOUR PASSIONS

—Page 30 extract is from 'Obsessions' from *Writing Down the Bones: Freeing the Writer Within* by Natalie Goldberg, © 1986 by Natalie Goldberg. Reprinted by arrangement with The Permissions Company, LLC on behalf of Shambhala Publications Inc., Boulder, Colorado, shambhala.com

12
YOU CAN BE ANYTHING YOU LIKE

—Page 37 extract is from 'Groundhog Day', © Charles Boyle (*Sonofabook* blog, www.cbeditions.com, Sunday 29 May 2011)

—Page 37 I'm thinking of Paul Auster's novel *Timbuktu*, Margaret Atwood's *The Handmaid's Tale*, Beryl Bainbridge's *The Birthday Boys* and Tom Robbins' *Skinny Legs and All*

14
WORD-WORLDS

—Page 40 examples are inspired by studying Anglo-Saxon (Old English) and reading *A History of the English Language*, © Albert C. Baugh and Thomas Cable (Routledge & Kegan Paul, 1951, revised 1978)

—Page 41 extract is © Simon Finberg, with kind permission

16
WRITE WHAT YOU KNOW?

—Page 45 Annie Proulx described researching and other creative processes during her Brighton Festival talk, 13 May 2001

17
RESEARCH IS A BEAUTIFUL PLACE

—Page 47 extract is from *The TV President*, © Elise Valmorbida (CB Editions, 2008, and BareBone Books, 2019)

18
SPEND, SPEND, SPEND

—Page 50–1 quotations are from William Shakespeare's *The Life and Death of King Richard II* (Act I, Scene 3 and Act V, Scene 5)

20
NOTHING IS WASTED

—Page 53 see *Lord of the Flies*, © William Golding (Faber & Faber, 1954). See also 'Strangers from Within', by Charles Monteith in *William Golding: The Man and His Books*, edited by John Carey (Faber & Faber, 1986)

22
POSSIBLY YOUR GREATEST TALENT

—Variations of the joke on page 56 are attributed to Peter Cook, Barry Fantoni and others. It's discussed in 'Time for Peter Cook to have the last laugh', an article by Judith Woods (the *Daily Telegraph*, 18 September 2012) and 'Satire's brightest star', an article by cartoonist Barry Fantoni (the *Guardian*, 10 January 1995)

23
PUT OFF PROCRASTINATION

—Page 59 see *The Salmon of Doubt: Hitchhiking the Galaxy One Last Time* © Douglas Adams (Penguin Random House, 2002)

24
THE CLOAK OF INVISIBILITY

—See 'An Interview with Dick Francis' in *The Dick Francis Companion*, Jean Swanson and Dean James (Berkley Prime Crime, 2003) pp.1–10

—Vincent van Gogh, Albert Einstein and Apple Inc. co-founder Steve Wozniak seem to have introversion in common. There's more about the power of shyness in Susan Cain's book *Quiet: The Power of Introverts in a World That Can't Stop Talking* (Penguin Random House, 2012)

26
IT MATTERS A WHOLE LOT

—Page 65 extract is from 'Against the Wall', © Marlene Dumas (David Zwirner Books, 2010) reprinted at Tate Modern, *Marlene Dumas: The Image as Burden* exhibition, 5 February–10 May 2015

27
READING LOVES WRITING LOVES READING

—Page 67 extract is from 'What Reading Does for the Mind', © Anne E. Cunningham and Keith E. Stanovich, *Journal of Direct Instruction*, Vol. 1, No. 2, pp.137–49, 2001, reprinted from *American Educator*, Vol. 22, No.1–2, pp.8–15, with kind permission of the authors

—Page 67 quotation is from 'Noble Science and Nobel Lust', a talk by Carl Djerassi at The British Library, London, 28 February 2006

28
THE PERFECT SPONGE

—Page 69 extract is from *Human, All Too Human: A Book for Free Spirits*, Friedrich Nietzsche, translation © R.J. Hollingdale (Cambridge University Press, 1986, 1996, reprinted 2003) pp.86–7

35
LOVE YOUR NOTEBOOK

—Page 83 extract is from 'On Keeping a Notebook', an essay in *Slouching Towards Bethlehem*, © Joan Didion (Farrar, Straus & Giroux, 1968, reprinted 4th Estate, 2017) pp.136 and 139

37
ETHICAL EAVESDROPPING

—Page 86 extract is © Claire Coleman, with kind permission

39
WAKE UP AND HEAR THE COFFEE

—Page 91 extract is from the poem 'Thirteen Ways of Looking at a Blackbird', *Selected Poems*, Wallace Stevens (Faber & Faber Ltd, 1953, reprinted 1980) p.44

—Page 91 references to Alfred Hitchcock's film *Psycho* are from a talk by Saul Bass at The Barbican Centre in London, spring 1986.

43
YOU NEED ONLY ONE VIOLIN

—Page 99 quotation is from *Notes on the Cinematographer*, © Robert Bresson (Éditions Gallimard, 1975), translation © Jonathan Griffin (Quartet Books, 1986) p.16, with kind permission of Jonathan Griffin's literary executor Anthony Rudolf

44
THE TRUTH ABOUT CLICHÉS

—Page 101 extracts are from *Sonnet 130*, William Shakespeare

—See 'Politics and the English Language' first published 1946, © the Estate of Sonia Brownell Orwell, 1984, reprinted in *Why I Write*, George Orwell (Penguin Books, 2004) pp.105–6

45
DESCRIBING WITHOUT DESCRIPTION

—Page 102–3 extract is © Ian Pring, with kind permission

46
ACTION THROUGH DESCRIPTION

—The essay that refers to the objective correlative is 'Hamlet and His Problems' from *The Sacred Wood: Essays on Poetry and Criticism*, T.S. Eliot (Methuen, 1920)

—John Gardner's creative writing exercise inspired by Eliot's essay is in *The Art of Fiction: Notes on Craft for Young Writers* (Alfred A. Knopf, 1983)

50
'I AM A WRITER'

—The line 'if you wish to be a writer, write' is from *Discourses*, Book II, 18, 1–2, Epictetus, Greek Stoic philosopher, *c.*55–135 AD. 'Every habit and ability is aided and increased by its corresponding action – the habit of walking, by walking; of running, by running. If you want to be a reader, read; if a writer, write.' Translation © Chris Hartney, with kind permission

58
CLASH OF THE TONGUES

—Page 133–4 see *Sarah*, © J.T. LeRoy (Bloomsbury, 2000)

—Page 134 see *When the Emperor was Divine*, © Julie Otsuka (Alfred A. Knopf, 2002)

59
A METAPHOR IS LIKE...

—Page 135 quotation is from the poem 'A Red, Red Rose', Robert Burns

—Page 135 quotation is from *Sonnet 18,* William Shakespeare

62
EUREKA MOMENTS
(LOVE YOUR UNCONSCIOUS)

—See Robert McCrum's article 'William Golding's Crisis' in *The Observer Magazine,* 11 March 2012

—Page 144 quotation is from 'Preface to the First Edition' in *Doctor Brodie's Report* © Jorge Luis Borges (Emecé Editores, 1970), translation © Norman Thomas di Giovanni in collaboration with the author (Dutton, 1972, reprinted Bantam Books, 1973) p.xi

—Page 144 extract is from *Dreamgates: An Explorer's Guide to the Worlds of Soul, Imagination, and Life Beyond Death,* © Robert Moss (Three Rivers Press, 1998) p.144, with kind permission of the author

—Page 144–5 extract is from *Manifeste du Surréalisme (Surrealist Manifesto),* André Breton (1924) translation by Elise Valmorbida

63
THE RICHES OF RANDOMNESS

—Karole Armitage was in London with her company performing *Drastic-Classicism* and *Two Theories: Quantum and String* as part of Dance Umbrella, 2011. I made notes after hearing her in interview (13 October 2011)

65
ABSOLUTE POWER
(LOVE YOUR INTELLECT)

—Those flies and wanton boys hail from William Shakespeare's *King Lear* (Act IV, Scene 1)

—See *Bagombo Snuff Box: Uncollected Short Fiction,* © Kurt Vonnegut (Jonathan Cape, 1999) p.10, or listen to the author voicing his 'Creative Writing 101' on www.youtube.com

68
BE A STUDENT FOREVER

—The 'four stages of competence' learning model traces its history through Martin M. Broadwell ('Teaching for learning', *The Gospel Guardian,* 1969), Paul R. Curtiss and Phillip W. Warren (*The Dynamics of Life Skills Coaching,* 1973) and Noel Burch at Gordon Training International ('four stages for learning any new skill', 1970s)

—Katsushika Hokusai wrote about ageing and achievement in the postscript to the first volume of his illustrated book *One Hundred Views of Mt Fuji.* His last spoken words, imagining five more years of life, were noted by his daughter Eijo

70
GROW YOUNGER

—See *The Man Who Mistook His Wife for a Hat and Other Clinical Tales,* © Oliver Sacks (Gerald Duckworth & Co, 1985, reprinted Pan Picador, 1986) p.13

—Page 163 extract is from 'Ode: Intimations of Immortality from Recollections of Early Childhood', William Wordsworth, first published in *Poems, in Two Volumes* (Longman, Hurst, Rees & Orme, 1807)

71
LOSE YOURSELF

—Page 165 extracts are from *Doctor Zhivago,* © Boris Pasternak (Feltrinelli, 1957), translation © Nicolas Pasternak Slater (The Folio Society, 2019) p.468

—Psychologist Mihaly Csikszentmihalyi identified and analyzed the mental state of 'flow', publishing studies from the 1970s onwards. See his book *Flow: The Psychology of Optimal Experience* (Harper & Row, 1990)

73
AN ARGUMENT FOR TRUTH

—Page 167 extract is from 'Place in Fiction', © Eudora Welty (1955), reprinted in *On Writing* (Modern Library Edition, 2002), p.40

—Page 168 extract is from *Journals 1889–1949,* André Gide (Penguin Books, 1967, reprinted 1978), first published by Alfred A. Knopf (1947), translation © Justin O'Brien (1947) p.23

74
PERSON-BUILDING

—Page 170 extract is from © Ben Marcus's interview with George Saunders (*The Believer,* Issue Eleven, 1 March 2004) quoted with kind permission of author, interviewer and publisher

75
YOUR DIARY WILL KEEP YOU

—Mae West's character Peaches O'Day (*Every Day's a Holiday*, 1937), actress Lillie Langtry, diarist Margot Asquith and a centuries-old proverb all inform the quip about your diary keeping you. See www.quoteinvestigator.com/2014/05/11/diary/

—Nawal El Saadawi was in conversation with Lisa Appignanesi at *Free the Word!* festival of literature organized by PEN International in London, 14–18 April 2010. I was a reporter at the festival, and co-led a crowd-writing project that highlighted 50 suppressed writers over 50 years. Another source of inspiration here: 'Nawal El Saadawi on feminism, fiction and the illusion of democracy', her interview with Krishnan Guru-Murthy (*Channel 4 News*, 'Ways to Change the World' podcast, 13 June 2018).

77
INVENT AN
ALTERNATIVE PRESENT

—Pages 175–6 extract is from the preface (31 July 2006) to *Dear Charlie: Letters to a Lost Daughter*, © Reg Thompson 2006 (John Murray, 2007) pp.ix–x, with kind permission of the author

78
WRITE THE FUTURE

—Page 178 extract is © Ezri Carlebach, with kind permission

—See 'Fantastic Beasts and How to Rank Them', © Kathryn Schulz, October 30, 2017 (published in *The New Yorker*, November 6, 2017 issue)

—The essay 'Why write?' from *Picked-Up Pieces*, © John Updike (Alfred A. Knopf, 1975), is reprinted in *Burn This Book*, edited by Toni Morrison (HarperCollins, 2009) p.15

79
FIND MATERIAL
IN MISFORTUNE

—Page 180 quotation is from *The Diary of Anaïs Nin, Vol. IV: 1944–1947*, © Anaïs Nin (Harcourt Brace, 1971) p.65

80
WRITE OUT THE NEGATIVE

—Page 181 quotation is often attributed to Maya Angelou, but it is from Zora Neale Hurston, *Dust Tracks on a Road* (J.B. Lippincott, 1942), © renewed 1970 by John C. Hurston, reprinted (HarperCollins, 1996) chapter XI 'Books and Things'

—I first came across James Pennebaker's work when I heard 'James Pennebaker and Expressive Writing' (BBC Radio 4, 12 April 2013), part of BBC Radio 4's *Mind Changers* series about the history of psychology, presented by Claudia Hammond

—Page 182 extract is from 'Sketch of the Past' in *Moments of Being*, Virginia Woolf (autobiographical writings, 18 April 1939–17 November 1940), © Quentin Bell and Angelica Garnett (Sussex University Press, 1976, reprinted Pimlico, 2002) p.85

81
WRITE UP THE POSITIVE

—Pages 183–4 extracts are from *The Book of Happy Endings*, © Elise Valmorbida (Cyan Books, 2007, and BareBone Books, 2014)

83
SEE MORE

—Page 188 see *Girl with a Pearl Earring*, © Tracy Chevalier (HarperCollins, 1999)

—Page 189 quotation is from *A Room of One's Own*, Virginia Woolf, (Hogarth Press/Harcourt Brace, 1929), © renewed Leonard Woolf, 1957, reprinted (The Folio Society, 2000) p.31

85
MAKE YOURSELF FEEL

—Page 192 quotation is from Gustave Flaubert's letter to Louise Colet [Croiset], Saturday night [24 April 1852], printed in *The Letters of Gustave Flaubert, 1830–1857*, translation © Francis Steegmuller (Harvard University Press, 1979, 1980) p.158

86
FEEL WITH OTHERS

—See Jason Baehr's 2012–15 e-book *Cultivating Good Minds: A Philosophical & Practical Guide to Educating for Intellectual Virtues*, (www.intellectualvirtues.org)

—See Simon Baron-Cohen's book *Zero Degrees of Empathy: A New Theory of Human Cruelty* (Penguin, 2011)

91
ALL CREATIVITY IS
GOOD FOR YOU

—Pages 204–5 quotation is © Tracey Loftis, with kind permission

—Page 205 extract is from *How to Change the World*, © John-Paul Flintoff (Pan Macmillan, 2012) p.76

93
IS IT PUBLISHABLE?

—Jonny Geller's talk 'What Makes a Bestseller?' (TEDxOxford, 2016) is well worth a listen. He talks about reading, storytelling, craft, agenting, publishing, marketing… See www.youtube.com

97
MAKE RIPPLES

—Page 217 extract is from *Orlando: A Biography*, Virginia Woolf (Hogarth Press, 1928) © Quentin Bell and Angelica Garnett, reprinted (Granada Publishing, 1977, 1982) p.108

—The poem 'Warning' © Jenny Joseph (1962; *Rose in the Afternoon*, J.M. Dent, 1974) inspired the founding in 1998 of the Red Hat Society, now an international social organization with a membership of 35,000+ women. See www.redhatsociety.com

98
CHANGE THE WORLD

—Page 219 extract is from *How to Change the World*, © John-Paul Flintoff (Pan Macmillan, 2012) p.51

—See *Silent Spring*, © Rachel Carson (Houghton Mifflin, 1962)

SOME HAPPY STORIES

—Page 226 extracts are © Chris Quinn, with kind permission

—Pages 226–7 extracts are from *The Book of Happy Endings*, © Elise Valmorbida (Cyan Books, 2007, and BareBone Books, 2014)

—Page 228 extract is © Geza Singer, with kind permission

Every reasonable effort has been made to identify owners of copyright. Errors or omissions will be corrected in subsequent editions.

ACKNOWLEDGEMENTS

Book backers

ZenAzzurrians, Clare Alexander, Sara Goldsmith, Jo Lightfoot, Elen Jones

Attentive readers

Annemarie Neary, Ian Gollan, Eve Aspinall, George O.

Happy storytellers

Claire Martin, Chris Quinn, Geza Singer

Workshop contributors

Simon Finberg, Claire Coleman, Ian Pring, Chris F., Guillem A., Takayo S., Yasmeen M., Khadiza L., Louise Fernley, Hetian Wang, Tracey Loftis and all those who sent me writings for this book

Contributors along the way

Glyn Williams (tai chi teachings), Denise Holmes (wise counsel), Nicolas Pasternak Slater (Zhivago), Ezri Carlebach (sci-fi mavenry), Sam Patterson (models, perseverance), Chris Hartney (Greek translation), Katsura Isobe (Japanese co-translation), Nadia Valmorbida (Latin co-translation), Claire Needham (that boat), Tara Wynne (faith)

Finishers

Charlotte Selby (editing), Harry Pearce (cover design)

My first teacher

Thank you for encouraging me to read and write, before and after the wallpaper

THE AUTHOR'S STORY

Writer-teacher Elise Valmorbida holds a first-class honours degree in English Language and Literature from the University of Melbourne, two teaching diplomas in Speech and Drama from Trinity College of Music London, and a first-class honours degree in Graphic Design from Central Saint Martins.

In her career as designer and creative director, Elise has worked with big brands and small, helping them to engage their audiences and communicate more effectively. She left corporate employment in 1997 and went on to set up her communications consultancy *word-design*, launch her first novel *Matilde Waltzing,* and teach Creative Writing at Central Saint Martins. She produced and script-consulted an award-winning microbudget feature film, for which she was honoured as an Edinburgh International Film Festival Trailblazer. Her non-fiction 'making of' story was published with the screenplay. For five years, Elise was External Examiner of Falmouth University's MA in Professional Writing and, in 2017, she was President of the D&AD Writing for Design jury. She is a member of English PEN and The Society of Authors, and a board director of Writers' Association 26.

Following the publication of *Matilde Waltzing, The Book of Happy Endings, The TV President* and *The Winding Stick,* her most recent work *The Madonna of the Mountains* was published internationally in several languages and won the Victorian Premier's Literary Award for fiction.

Elise continues to teach Creative Writing at Central Saint Martins, Arvon Foundation, Faber Academy, Guardian Masterclasses, literary festivals and community-building organizations. She mentors individuals and corporate teams, and co-leads workshops on creative writing and wellbeing.

The Happy Writing Book is the result of decades of deliberation and discovery about the art, craft and positive experience of creative writing.